VIETNAM WAR
50TH ANNIVERSARY MEMOIRS

AS WRITTEN BY
CALIFORNIA DAR DAUGHTERS

CALIFORNIA STATE SOCIETY
DAUGHTERS OF THE AMERICAN REVOLUTION
GLENDORA, CA

COMPILED BY SALLY J. HOLCOMBE
CSSDAR HISTORIAN, 2014-2016

Vietnam War Memoirs as Written by California DAR Daughters
California State Society Daughters of the American Revolution
Sally J. Holcombe, Compiler

ISBN-10: 1514275880
ISBN-13: 978-1514275887

First Edition.
Printed in the United States of America.

Layout by Sally J. Holcombe, CSSDAR State Historian
Anne Loucks Chapter, NSDAR, Martinez, California

Cover, title page and back cover designs by Jeanette Hacker
Beverly Hills Chapter, NSDAR, Beverly Hills, California

Library of Congress Control Number: 2015910659
CreateSpace Independent Publishing Platform, North Charleston, SC

To commemorate the 50th Anniversary
of the Vietnam War; to honor and thank
the servicemen and women who served so bravely
and the people on the home front
who waited - and continue to wait - for their return.

CONTENTS

i

STATE REGENT'S MESSAGE

By Carol Oakley Jackson, State Regent, 2014-2016
California State Society Daughters of the American Revolution

The National Society Daughters of the American Revolution (NS-DAR) is proud to be a partner with the Vietnam War 50th Anniversary Commemoration, a committee established by the United States Congress. Among the objectives of the program are to honor and thank veterans of the Vietnam War and to pay tribute to the contributions of those on the United States home front.

The California State Society (CSSDAR) became a Commemorative Partner and has encouraged its chapters to make application and participate as well. It is our opportunity to recognize Vietnam veterans and their families, as well as honor the memory of those no longer with us, for their service and sacrifice.

As a part of our participation, this book of memoirs of our California Daughters from that era, 1963-1974, presents the many different aspects of the experience, ones that also kept changing, of what we call the Vietnam War - a kaleidoscope of sorts. The experiences are like fingerprints, no two are alike.

For those of us who lived during that time, may we appreciate each story. For those who have only heard of that time, may this collection provide insight into a time of markedly different points of view. For all of us, may it provide a bridge between us and aid in the healing process.

PREFACE

By Sally J. Holcombe, State Historian, 2014-2016
California State Society Daughters of the American Revolution

The idea for a published collection of California DAR Daughters' Vietnam War memoirs was born at the 2014 CSSDAR State Conference. I was stationed at an exhibit table, promoting the partnership between the NSDAR and our nation's Vietnam War 50th Anniversary Commemoration Committee. Throughout the five-day meeting, California DAR Daughters stopped by and shared their Vietnam War experiences. I realized their stories deserved to be recorded, much like the stories being preserved via the Veterans' History Project (Library of Congress).

Once the project was approved by the CSSDAR State Board of Directors, a call went out to all California Daughters who experienced the Vietnam era. The resulting stories are preserved in this collection. A sincere attempt has been made to spell Vietnam place names correctly and to accurately identify military units, battles, events, ranks and awards. We apologize to military members if we have not achieved that goal. These are the personal memories of DAR Daughters, many of whom were not directly involved in the war.

Appreciation is extended to the CSSDAR State Board of Directors for approving this project, to the DAR Daughters who submitted their stories, and to the project committee members for their hard work. A special thank you to Jeanette Hacker for her cover design, and to Muriel Crawford for her expert advice. Finally, my deepest gratitude to my husband, Jerry Holcombe, for executing the final edit.

PROJECT COMMITTEE

Sally J. Holcombe, Committee Chair - A retired home economics and science educator, Sally is a graduate of Cal Poly, San Luis Obispo, California, with an M.S. Degree in Science Curriculum Development. She has been a DAR member since 2001 and currently serves as State Historian. She and husband, Jerry, reside in Walnut Creek, California. They have a son and daughter and three granddaughters. She volunteers as an officer for the Sacramento Valley National Cemetery Support Committee, as a Walnut Creek Police Department volunteer and as an officer for two lineage societies.

Francis Bock - Fran lives in Palos Verdes Estates, California. A 1965 DAR Good Citizen Award recipient, she graduated from North Texas State University with a B.A. in Music. She provided English and music instruction at Torrance High School, Torrence, California. She joined the DAR in 2005 and has served at the chapter and state levels. She and husband, Russell, have two daughters and two granddaughters.

Kathi Chulick - Kathi and her husband, John, have lived in several locations, currently residing in Montecito, California. A retired history teacher, Kathi holds a B.A. Degree in history from the University of Missouri. She and John have one daughter. Kathi has served the DAR at the chapter, district, and state levels. In addition to the DAR, she belongs to eight other lineage societies.

Muriel Crawford - A DAR member since 2005, Muriel is a published author of textbooks and nonfiction. She holds a B.A. Degree in English Literature from the University of Illinois and her *Juris Doctor* from the Chicago-Kent College of Law. She was House Counsel for the Life and Health Insurance Company. Muriel and husband, Barry, live in Walnut Creek, California. They have three daughters and five grandsons.

Michelle Field - Michelle is a California native, born and raised in Los Angeles. She has a degree in apparel merchandising and marketing and is currently working as a royalty analyst for a financial firm that caters to the entertainment industry. She joined Don José de Ortega Chapter, NSDAR as a Junior in 2012 and is her chapter's Historian. She also chairs several chapter committees and serves as a State Page.

Jeanette Hacker - Jeanette grew up in Highland, Indiana. She graduated from Columbia College Chicago, and works in Los Angeles on films and documentaries. She is a William Faulkner-Wisdom Creative Writing Competition finalist (novel category, 2014), and was a poetry semi-finalist in 2010. Jeanette joined Beverly Hills Chapter, NSDAR as a Junior in 2013. She is her chapter's 1st Vice Regent, chairs a committee and is a State Page.

Adina Roberts - A DAR member since 2004, Adina was a Data Center Manager and Business Continuity professional. She credits the DAR with providing opportunities for personal growth and leadership. Her activities included being a soccer and volleyball coach, as well as leading a Girl Scout troop for 13 years. She and her husband, William, reside in Pasadena, California. They have two daughters and two grandchildren.

OUR MARINES

By Joanne "Joedy" Adams
Linares Chapter, NSDAR
San Diego, California

It was June 1967. Little League season had ended, and our Little League was trying to expand to add more playing fields. Both of my sons were in Little League, and their father was very involved in the league. The San Diego City Council had just ruled that the league could expand onto school property. The elementary school adjacent to the field could use the fields during the school week while the Little League could maintain the fields and have them after school and on weekends. This meant the Little League would have to build the baseball fields.

One of the Little League board members was a retired Marine. He suggested that we approach the Marine Corps Recruit Depot (MCRD) to see if we could recruit volunteers to help. We needed strong, young bodies to do the hard work of preparing the grounds. This meant breaking up the blacktop to clear the way for grass. The MCRD's C & E battalions gave us permission to post a request, asking for volunteers to serve the Little League on Saturdays. I was tasked with following up on the post that first Saturday to see if there was anyone who was interested. I drove my Volkswagon bus, figuring it would suffice if I were able to recruit two or three Marines.

I had a big surprise when I arrived at the depot. I had to make *three* trips with my bus, and another lady helped out with transporting the rest! The Marines ran the tractors, did all the heavy work, and wouldn't let anyone else do it. The school opened up its cafeteria, and we served them Sloppy Joe sandwiches. The local liquor store furnished sodas and beer.

After a few weeks, we got to know some of the Marines and began having them at our home for the weekends. One weekend, we had seven Marines at the house...I had wall-to-wall Marines! They were so glad to be off base for a change. I had two conditions if they stayed with us: 1) they had to call their mothers sometime during the weekend; 2) if they were churchgoers, they would still attend. I planned to work out a schedule with our car so they could get there. By the time the field was ready, we had come to know about five of the Marines really well. Even after the field was done, those five Marines spent every weekend with us until they received their orders to go to Vietnam.

We told them we couldn't offer much in the way of fancy food, but they didn't mind. We ate a lot of tuna sandwiches and macaroni and cheese. We took them to the beach and left them to enjoy themselves. They loved it, especially the girls in bathing suits parading up and down the beach! Most of them were only 18 years old, and a few were 19.

We have a big, round dining table, so evenings were often spent playing cards. One night we made homemade ice cream. One of the Marines, Ed, had never done that. He offered to turn the paddles, and I told him, "He who does the work gets to lick the paddles." Well, he went to it and enjoyed the ice cream off the paddles. I can still see Ed, sitting there on my kitchen floor licking those paddles!

Getting ready for church the night before was really something to behold. There were usually about four Marines polishing their shoes, and taking turns using the ironing board to press their pants and shirts. Their mothers would have been proud.

My oldest son had his first school dance and was taking a neighbor. One Marine, Kevin, showed him how to open the car door for her and how to treat a lady. He drove them to the dance and picked them up afterwards. My son did not want his mother to drive him, so having a Marine chauffeur him was icing on the cake.

When we asked them why they signed up to help the Little League they said, "If we were home, we would be helping our younger brothers and sisters with their projects and supporting their events." Serving our community made them feel closer to home.

All of the Marines that we got to know went to Vietnam, and everyone of them returned safely home. I was a Girl Scout leader and had a troop at that time. Each month, we would send our Marines boxes of goodies.

We still correspond with three of them. One lives in Oregon, one in Missouri, and the other one in Massachusetts. They are all grandparents now, but they have never forgotten us, nor will we ever forget them. *Semper Fi!*

4

THE VIETNAM WAR IN BERKELEY

By Lindy McLaughlin Allen
General John A. Sutter Chapter, NSDAR
Sacramento, California

My first remembrance of the Vietnam War centered around my father's work for Kaiser Aluminum in the mid-1960's. He was in charge of new product development for Kaiser Aluminum in Oakland, and they had been asked to develop and improve a waterproof and dustproof landing mat for use in Vietnam. I remember my father getting FBI clearance to work on this fairly top-secret project. He never talked about what he was developing until after the project was completed.

The landing mat was a honeycomb structure that could be shipped in relatively lightweight packages to Vietnam and pieced together to make a large landing strip for planes in the jungle. My father won an achievement award from Kaiser for his contribution to this MX19 Landing Mat Program. I have the trophy piece of the mat that was given to him in a ceremony afterwards.

The piece of honeycomb landing mat (developed by Kaiser Aluminum and Chemical Company, Oakland, California) that was presented to Linda McLaughlin's father. This material was used to create portable landing strips during the Vietnam War.

I went to the University of California at Berkeley (beginning in 1967 and graduating in 1971) and was there on campus for all the antiwar protests that took place in 1969 and 1970. Although I was not a participant, there was no way to avoid the riots if you continued to go to class. Even then, I wondered just how many of the rioters were actually students at Cal, and how many were there just to take part in the demonstrations.

I remember walking to class through Sather Gate by the Student Union building, and all of a sudden having masses of people running towards me, chased by either the National Guard or by police throwing tear gas canisters. I could not turn and run because it would make me appear to actually be part of the protest, so I had to stroll quickly away and find an alternate route to class.

I worked part time in Swenson's Ice Cream Shop, just a block off of Telegraph Avenue and two blocks from Sather Gate. The National Guard or the police lined the streets. I had a checking account at the Bank of America right across from campus on Telegraph Avenue. I was actually inside the bank when the metal gates came down to lock us all inside to avoid the riot that made its way to our area.

In May, 1970, University of California students paralyzed the campus with massive riots. Then Governor Ronald Reagan decided to close the school. Whatever classes you were taking, whether part of your major or not, were changed to pass/fail grading and no finals were given. Class grades were based on work to that point. Although I did not graduate that year, senior graduation was cancelled for the first time in school history. Our *Blue and Gold* school yearbook, a tradition for over 100 years at the University of California, Berkeley, was renamed the *Tabula Rasa*. There were no pictures of classmates as there always had been.

The effects were still being felt when I graduated the following year. The big graduation ceremony still wasn't being held. Each school - mine being anthropology - held small, separate ceremonies.

To this day, I wonder just how many of the protestors were students. I have since read that the large majority were from outside campus.

TWO YEARS AS A FLIGHT NURSE

By Carol Anders
Captain Henry Sweetser Chapter, NSDAR
Santa Maria, California

"I was tired for two years," is how I used to describe my two years as a flight nurse during the Vietnam War. Please allow me to explain.

It all began while I was a captain in the United States Air Force Nurse Corps, assigned as an operating room nurse at Wilford Hall Hospital in San Antonio, Texas. I decided to volunteer for flight nurse school at Brooks Air Force Base, also in San Antonio. It was a six-week course teaching the particulars of caring for patients during aeromedical evacuation (medevac) flights. After graduating in 1965 from the school where I earned my coveted silver flight nurse wings to wear on my uniform, I was happy to go back to my work in the operating room. However, during that time an increasing number of soldiers wounded in Vietnam needed to be evacuated to stateside hospitals. In May of 1966, I received orders assigning me to the 56th Aeromedical Evacuation Squadron (AES) for two years of flight duty at Yokota Air Base, Japan.

Carol Anders at flight nurse training.

Living in Japan was quite a change for this Minnesota farm girl. I had my own tiny apartment in the Bachelor Officer Quarters (BOQ) at Tachikawa Air Base. It was about an hour train ride to Tokyo for shopping and sightseeing during time-off duty. My 56th AES at Yokota Air Base was a short drive from Tachikawa. Yes, I learned to drive it myself - on the left side of the road. I traveled that road so often it seemed like I spent more time going on trips than I did living in Japan. Often I would have only enough time there to get laundry done and repack for the next journey.

Our mission at the 56ᵗʰ AES was to fly from Yokota, Japan on board C-141 aircraft, to pick up wounded soldiers in Vietnam and bring them to base hospitals stateside for further treatment. Our medical crews usually consisted of two flight nurses and three medical technicians. Occasionally we would be lucky enough to have a physician on board. A normal patient load would be about thirty patients on litters and ten to fifteen ambulatory patients.

Since we flew two different routes to deliver patients to base hospitals closest to their homes, I had the opportunity to visit diverse areas of the world. Those who were from states east of the Mississippi River were flown from Vietnam to Japan, then to Alaska and on to bases on the East Coast. Those patients from west of the Mississippi were flown the southern route from Vietnam to the Philippines, from there to Hawaii and on to Travis Air Force Base, California.

The C-141 aircraft were huge cargo planes. They arrived from the United States packed with supplies that needed to be off-loaded

before our medical technicians could reconfigure the plane for our medevac flights. They loaded a "comfort pallet" which was a bathroom slightly larger than those on today's commercial airplanes. On my first couple of flights, I spent a lot of time in those bathrooms until I gained my "air legs." The supply crew

C-141 aircraft with rear clamshell doors open.

also brought on a small kitchen so that we could serve coffee to our patients and heat their frozen dinners. Even with those amenities, it was still a noisy, unevenly heated, sometimes rough ride, although the flight crew did their best to keep the flights as smooth and comfortable as possible. There were only a couple of portholes in the back of the aircraft so it was almost impossible to view the world outside.

Our destinations in Vietnam were Cam Ranh Bay, Da Nang or Tan Son Nhut Air Bases where buses with patients from the field hospitals would be waiting for us. The buses were able to back up through the open rear clamshell doors of the C-141. This allowed the medical technicians to carry the litter patients directly from the buses onto the aircraft where they would secure the litters to brackets on the walls, straps or center stanchions of the aircraft. Many patients had bulky bandages or casts, some would have intravenous infusions running, most would need medications during the flight.

Off-loading a patient onto the ambulance bus.

At times the litter patients would be stacked three deep so that it was not possible for them to sit up comfortably, and they needed help to eat. As uncomfortable as our patients might be, they were just so happy to be heading home!

During the Tet Offensive of 1968, all leaves, including mine, were cancelled. I had planned to attend the ice festival in Sapporo, Japan, but all medical flight crews were needed to move patients out of Vietnam. Flight nurses and medical technicians from assignments in Europe and Air National Guard personnel were sent TDY (temporary duty) to supplement our crews. On one of my flights into Tan Son Nhut Air Base, Saigon, the air traffic was so heavy the flight crew asked volunteers from the medical crew to come up to the cockpit to help spot aircraft while we were on landing approach. From the cockpit, I could see the spirals of barbed wire in the sand dunes alongside the runway. It was a chilling sight.

When flying into Da Nang, the medical crew usually remained on board during the brief stop. During one of those trips, I had a chance to debark and walk around the tent city. It looked like something out of the *MASH* television series, made more sobering by the sound of artillery fire in the distance.

I felt safer on our flights into Cam Ranh Bay. We jokingly said we were going for Rest & Recreation (R&R). On some occasions we would stay overnight in the nurses' quarters on the base and spend time at the beautiful beaches.

Cam Ranh Bay, Vietnam.

One of my flights consisted of all heavily-bandaged burn patients on their way to the burn unit at Brooke Army Medical Center, San Antonio. For this flight, an extra medical crew was assigned because there was no crew change en route from Vietnam to San Antonio. Only refueling stops and change of flight crew were made. With an extra medical crew on board, we took turns resting and sleeping when possible. All patients had intravenous infusions running and needed lots of pain medication. While saddened by their condition, I knew they would be getting the best possible care at Brooke Army Medical Center.

In spite of the long, tiring flights, it was an opportunity to visit parts of the world I would not have seen otherwise. It was challenging but rewarding duty. I definitely earned the privilege of wearing silver wings on my uniforms for the rest of my Air Force career.

THE SHIMMERONS

By Carol McBride Anderson
Monserate Chapter, NSDAR
Fallbrook, California

"NEWS FROM USO SHOWS
USO SHOWS #GS-1018 Pacific Hospital Circuit
'THE SHIMMERONS,' the 1970-71 'Sweethearts of Harmony,'
will entertain at Pacific Hospitals starting 16 September 1971.
Their songs will cheer Vietnam veterans in hospitals in Japan,
Guam, Okinawa and the Philippines. The 17-day tour is sponsored
by USO, Sweet Adelines, Inc. and the Department of Defense. 'The
Shimmerons' were organized in December of '69 and won their
first title at the Biltmore Bowl in April 1970 – representing Region
#11 Southern California, Arizona and Nevada. The quartet has sung
with Lawrence Welk, the Steve Allen Show, at Knott's Berry Farm,
Disneyland, many civic clubs and for TV commercials."

In 1971, my barbershop quartet, "The Shimmerons," was honored
to be invited to entertain the troops on the USO tour. Our quartet
was made up of four voices. My name is Carol Anderson, and I
sang lead along with Suzy McGehee, tenor; Valerie Peter, baritone;
and Shirley Rice, bass. We were members of the Sweet Adelines
International organization.

We were told we would either have orders to go to Vietnam or to
the Far East. As it was, we were given a travel itinerary for the Far
East that included entertaining in four countries: Japan, Philippines,
Guam, and Okinawa. It was a challenge for me to be able to go on
a three-week trip away from my family. I was divorced at the time,
working a brand new job, and had three children: Larry, age ten,
Christine, nine, and Debra, seven. My wonderful mother and my
ex-husband agreed to care for the children while I was away. What
a blessing! I told my boss that this was a chance in a lifetime, and
I couldn't miss this opportunity. Luckily, my job was held for my
return.

Excitement was in the air as we departed on our journey, September 14, 1971, for our first stop in Tokyo, Japan.

We flew out of Los Angeles International Airport to San Francisco International Airport and on to Honolulu, Hawaii. The last leg of this first journey was seven hours to Tokyo, Japan. Halfway through the flight, the quartet surprised me with an Oreo cookie and a candle they obtained from the stewardesses. They sang "Happy Birthday" to me, in celebration of my 30th birthday.

We were originally scheduled on an Air Force flight out of Travis Air Force Base, but the flight was cancelled. We flew Northwest Orient Airlines instead. That caused a delay in customs at the Tokyo airport, but we finally passed inspection along with our seventeen pieces of luggage. We arrived at the Sanno Hotel in Toyko and settled into our room for the night and some much needed sleep.

The next day, September 16th, was our first day to entertain at the base hospital outside of Tokyo. We were picked up at 11 a.m. Our destination was the Army Hospital at Zama Army Base, 25 miles from Tokyo. Once there, we met the Red Cross representative and were given the schedule for the day. We entertained the troops on every floor throughout the hospital, going into each ward, one at a time, singing songs like: "Over There," "He's Got the Whole World in His Hands," "Mr. Sandman," "Raindrops Keep Falling on My Head," "Young and Foolish," and many others. The men's morale was very high, and they were a joy to sing to.

We were told that the worst burn cases were airlifted directly from Vietnam to this hospital. The head of the burn unit came to us and asked if we would sing in his ward. The Red Cross said we didn't have to - it was our choice - but we said, "After all, that's why we are here, to sing for the wounded." Our bass vocalist had been a nurse, and she said that we would be able to handle it. So, of course, we did. We had to put on some "lovely" white gowns and the booties, and could not take anything else into the ward with us.

As we entered the room, all the men's beds were tented because of their burns. We were unable to see their faces. We went to the end of each hospital bed and just started singing. One of my favorite songs then and now is "Mr. Sandman." As we were singing, we could see the men tapping their toes on the end of their beds, beating to the rhythm of our music. We went on from bed to bed singing for each patient. One good thing is that the men could not see the tears streaming down our faces, but we kept singing. When we finished working our way around the room, the head physician came to us and told us that one of the patients who had been tapping his toes to our music had not responded previously to anything until we sang for him. That one patient made our whole trip worthwhile. I could tell you many more stories about things that happened as we went from one country to another. However, this one moment meant the most to me and it always will.

God bless our veterans, and God bless America!

The "Shimmerons" and others, left to right: Suzy McGehee, audience member, Carol Anderson, Valerie Peters, hospital staff member, Shirley Rice.

MY HUSBAND'S TOUR OF DUTY

By Retha Anderson
Feather River Chapter, NSDAR
Oroville, California

My husband, Norris Eugene "Gene" Anderson, served in Vietnam from April 1968 to December 1969. We started dating just before he left for training at Davis Monthan Air Force Base. Shortly after completing training, he was sent to Vietnam. His first base in Vietnam was Da Nang Air Force Base. He was there for thirteen months, after which he came home on leave to be married. He had to attend pre-marriage counseling classes and sent me little pamphlets to read before the Air Force would approve our getting married.

Retha and Gene Anderson.

We rented a small apartment that adjoined the owner's house. Our rent was $55 per month and included utilities. Gene went back to Vietnam for another six months, and I lived on $100 per month. I was able to pay rent, buy food, and even put some money into savings. Times were pretty good.

The bad part was seeing the news on television each night when broadcasts showed the war and the bodies of our fallen soldiers. Sometimes, this was how loved ones found out their husbands or sons were dead. The networks were so busy making sure the war was covered publicly, that they did not care how what they were showing might affect loved ones at home. I did not watch the news very much.

We wrote letters to each other almost every single night. His were more like novels, sometimes twelve pages long. He described his everyday life on base and all the terrible things that were happening. One time, the F-4 Phantom for which he was the crew chief, crashed into a mountain and lost both pilots. Gene had to go before a military review board to see if he was responsible for the pilots' deaths. He was found not at fault.

Another time, one of his planes crashed on landing. When pilots were coming in for a landing, they would empty the plane's fuel tanks prior to touchdown. One tank malfunctioned, failed to empty and caused the plane to be unbalanced. The plane flipped over, crashed on the runway and trapped one man underneath. The other man ejected into jet fuel and was burned over 70% of his body. He lived for a time but finally died. This was a very hard time for my husband.

Gene was so tired most nights that one night, he slept through an air raid siren. His roommates could not wake him, so they rolled him under the bottom bunk and went on to the shelter. It was common for him to sleep in his flack jacket after that night.

He said he frequently smelled marijuana being smoked around base, so he knew about it. Growing up in the country where we did, neither of us had ever heard of party drugs before. Lots of the men came home addicted to marijuana and worse things.

Gene came home to stay in December, 1969, at which time we were assigned to Mountain Home Air Force Base in Idaho. For the most part, non-military people treated our men as if they had the plague or were murderers. Gene didn't wear his uniform off base, so he did not experience much of that personally.

While at Mountain Home, Gene was once again working on F-4 Phantoms. We were able to get base housing which was not bad. It did have lead paint that was peeling off the baseboards in most places. Things were not going too badly for us personally as far as the war was concerned. Then "Hanoi Jane" Fonda decided to show up and tried to cause riots on base. She went to downtown Mountain Home and had little rallies to try to get the airmen to picket the base. Some did. This caused the base to put armed airmen at the gates. One of those men was my husband who personally knew some of the young guys. He was told to shoot them if they came onto the base. He wasn't sure he could shoot another airman with whom he worked on a daily basis. Thankfully, he did not have to make that decision because those young airmen decided they did not want to get shot either. My husband and many others will never forgive Jane Fonda for the things she did during those years.

The one and only time I have ever seen my husband cry was when they were showing the Vietnam War Memorial on television. As his wife, that was very hard to see. So how did the Vietnam War affect me? I did not lose my husband or family member. I did not have a wounded man come home, unless you count his uncontrolled anger from time to time. I did lose some friends and school friends. Some died there, another died from Agent Orange which, among other things, caused leukemia. The military denied being at fault to his family, and they didn't even receive one dime to help with his medical expenses.

After all these years, my husband and others like him are just now being recognized for their Vietnam War service. They were not welcomed home as heroes. Their lives were altered just as other war heroes' lives were altered, but they were not treated in the same way other war heroes were treated.

I was young and somewhat ignorant in the ways of the world. I didn't realize just how much of an impact this would have on my family. We have two children. When they were growing up, there were people who tried to shame them because their dad served in Vietnam. One was a minister who told them they should be ashamed of their father for fighting in Vietnam in the way he did - for doing what his country asked of him. We left that church. My children are proud of their dad and his military service. My grandsons are being taught just how important men like Gene really are. They are being taught to be proud of their country and of the men who have fought for her since her beginnings.

My husband, Gene, was in the Air Force for eleven and a half years. He finished up his twenty years for retirement in the Army National Guard.

THE HANDSOME LIEUTENANT

By Joyce Deatherage Bayne
Merced River Chapter, NSDAR
Merced, California

Empty Runway...No B-52, No KC-135
Vacant Ramp, No Vehicles, No Personnel
They were gone. All were gone. My husband was gone.
To where? How long? Why? What I was to do now?

These are my memories of the Vietnam War. I was the bride of a
1st Lieutenant at Barksdale Air Force Base, Louisiana. He was a
navigator on the B-52 bomber. I was learning a new language, an
Air Force language: alert, claxon, TDY, security, regulations, commissary, leave. And now, there were new words: Guam, Anderson,
missiles.

February 1965, the entire Air Force Wing flew out of the United
States on a secret mission to a secret location. My husband returned
three months later, and we moved to Texas the following month. I
thought - we thought - he would stay stateside, but two months later,
he was gone again. Our first child was born while he was gone. I
stayed alone in our first house with a new baby.

The world now knew about Vietnam and the bombing of the North.
I was proud of my husband, but many people were beginning to
object. I removed our name plate, which included his rank, from
our address. To strangers I just said he was away working. I was
fortunate to have support from my family and my church. Other
wives did not. Some brides returned to their parents, others pursued
careers, or continued their education. Regretfully, some marriages
failed.

I learned how to adjust. The dream of a husband always by my side
morphed into the reality of me being alone and having to be both
the mother and the head of household. I wanted to be a *wife* and
mother.

In the next five years, my husband was sent TDY (temporary duty) four more times. We had two more boys. We moved two more times before he was told he was now surplus. The B-52 bomber was being deactivated. My husband would no longer be needed. He thought he was going to have a military career. He returned to civilian life and I stood by my husband. Yes, life was hard, but meaningful. We were doing a job for our country.

I never took a political stand on the Vietnam War. I was, and am, a patriot. I did not confront people who were against the war. History has recorded all the opposition. I wanted to tell how I, and thousands of wives like me, accepted the hardships of war.

I am still married to my handsome lieutenant. We recently celebrated our golden wedding anniversary. He still goes to work every day at his own business, and I am now "Grandma."

CLOSURE

By Anita Bell
Los Gatos Chapter, NSDAR
Los Gatos, California

My youngest brother, Gordon Lee Page, was born in Palo Alto, California, on August 15, 1932. Our middle brother was named Willard. Our parents were Forrest Page and Laura Van Wie Page. I was four and a half years old when Gordon was born. I loved being his "second mother." He was a cutie and a lot of fun to be with.

When Gordon was older, he enjoyed making and playing with model airplanes. He graduated from Sequoia High School in Redwood City, California, and from the College of San Mateo. I wasn't surprised when he joined the Air Force. He was commissioned in the Air Force at Vance Air Force Base, Oklahoma. He received his wings and married his lovely wife, Lou Leusley, on the same day - December 16, 1953. I really enjoyed Lou, and my children had fun with their cousins. It was great to see them when they flew into Moffett Field on leave.

For a time, Gordon was stationed at Hamilton Air Force Base in Marin County, California. He was sent to Udorn Royal Thai Air Force Base, Thailand, and assigned to Rolling Thunder. His mission was to identify possible bombing targets and to take post-raid photos of bombed areas in North Vietnam. On March 7, 1966, he and his wing man took off in their unarmed RF-101C Voodoo photo reconnaissance jet. Later, several radar stations received distress calls from an unidentified pilot who said his aircraft had been struck by a missile. There was no further contact, and a search yielded nothing.

A serviceman contacted my husband at his place of employment to tell him about Gordon's plane being shot down over Vietnam. I will never forget that day when he came home to tell me the sad news. We drove to Palo Alto to comfort my folks. My father had been home to receive the news from a serviceman, and he contacted a pastor to help him tell my mother when she came home from her place of employment. It was a difficult time. My mother had hope, because Gordon was listed as "Missing in Action" rather than being "Killed in Action." We then contacted Gordon's family members to be with them during their suffering. He and his wingman were listed as "Missing in Action" for eight years. It was sad, and we all lived those many years without closure, without knowing. During that time, Gordon was promoted to colonel.

On June 1, 1989, the Socialist Republic of Vietnam turned over twenty-eight boxes of remains to the United States. These were sent to Hawaii to the United States Army Central Identification Laboratory. It was presumed that Gordon had been buried in a backyard near the crash site and that his body was exhumed by representatives of the District Military Command. Officials identified him using dental charts and DNA samples from his niece and me. Pathologists determined a probable match.

Our country has a goal of bringing home all its warriors from combat. Gordon's remains, cased in a silver-colored military casket, were escorted from Hawaii by Air Force Colonel George Bowen and attended by a twenty-two-member Honor Guard from Beale Air Force Base. He was laid to rest at Paradise Cemetery in Paradise, California. Active duty military and civilians attended the funeral and graveside service, complete with full military honors. His widow, Lou, accepted the flag from his casket with cartridges from the three-volley final salute wrapped inside and his medals pinned to the presentation box. We had all waited thirty-two years for that day.

Memories are intact. Gordon's widow, Lou, daughter, Julie, and son, Jeff, remember the knock on their door at 4:00 a.m., March 7, 1966, in Okinawa military housing where they lived. Lou was two months pregnant with their second son, Gordon Scott Page, Jr., called "Chip." Chip never met his father.

Colonel Gordon Page was thirty-three years old when he died. He is survived by three children, five grandchildren; and by me, his sister, Anita Bell, of Los Gatos. His widow, Lou Page, of Paradise, California, and brother, Willard Page, of Tahoe City, California, have since passed away. The family feels closure. Gordon is finally at home!

Article published in the *San Jose Mercury News*, Wednesday, May 7, 1998.

G. Page, pilot killed in 1966, to be buried

BY MACK LUNDSTROM
Mercury News Staff Writer

A squad of Air Force jets will fly by and rifles will report 21 times at the veterans section of the Paradise cemetery on Friday, and Lou Page will finally bury her husband.

She waited 32 years.

Col. Gordon L. Page, a photo-reconnaissance pilot born in Palo Alto, disappeared on a flight over North Vietnam on March 7, 1966. His unarmed RF-101c didn't return to its base in Thailand.

Officers awakened Lou Page the next morning in Okinawa to say her husband was missing. Married 13 years, she had two children and was pregnant with her third.

In the next three decades, she moved to San Jose, reared her children and devoted much of her time advocating for the families of service men and women missing in action or taken prisoner.

And she repeatedly found cause to wonder — when a report would hint American prisoners were seen in North Vietnam, when pictures were published and later found to be bogus. "It was always something."

Demanded disclosure

For the National League for Families of American Prisoners in Southeast Asia, she paid her own way to Switzerland to demand that North Vietnam live up to the Geneva Convention and reveal the names of prisoners and the dead.

The limbo in which Lou Page called herself neither wife nor widow ended in April when she received a thick report detailing how DNA tests had confirmed that bones buried near a crash site, then reburied for safekeeping and finally shipped to Hawaii, were her husband's.

In the death of Col. Page, his wife has been brought to at least two closures that really weren't, she said Thursday.

In 1974, a presumptive finding was issued declaring Col. Page dead. A memorial service was held and a sapling was planted in what was then Plaza Park on Market Street in downtown San Jose. A

Gordon L. Page

- **Born:** Aug. 15, 1932, Palo Alto, Calif.
- **Died:** March 7, 1966, North Vietnam.
- **Survived by:** Wife, Lou Page of Paradise; sons, Jeffrey Page of San Francisco, Gordon Scott "Chip" Page of Paradise; daughter, Julie Page Ales of Aptos; sister, Anita Bell of Los Gatos; brother, Willard Page of Tahoe City; grandchildren, Kristen and Erica Ales of Aptos, Courtney, Trevor and Haley Page of Owosso, Mich.
- **Services:** Memorial at 1 p.m. Friday at Paradise Lutheran Church, burial with military honors following in veterans section of Paradise Cemetery.
- **Memorial:** Donations may be made to the Red River Valley Fighter Pilots' Association Scholarship Fund, Box 1551, North Fork, Calif. 93643 or the Paradise Lutheran Church Building Fund, 780 Luther Drive, Paradise, Calif. 95969.

plaque read "The Freedom Tree: With the Vision of Universal Freedom For All Mankind, This Tree Is Dedicated to Lt. Col. Gordon L. Page and All Prisoners of War And Missing in Action."

In 1989, North Vietnam shipped 28 boxes of remains to the U.S. Army Central Identification Center in Hawaii. Among them were those of Col. Page's wingman, identified by dental records, but Col. Page's remained unverified. That October, a workman discovered the plaque honoring Col. Page by its uprooted tree in what would become today's Cesar Chavez Park. Col. Page's plaque was rededicated at the north end of the park.

Interviews in Vietnam

In the next eight years, the ID center's personnel returned to Vietnam for interviews — with either "very, very old villagers or very, very young ones in 1966," Lou Page said.

The researchers found a Hanoi newspaper clipping detailing how "air pirates" had been shot down March 7, 1966.

Finally DNA samples from Col. Page's sister and niece confirmed

his identity.

Gordon Page grew up the son of Forest and Laura Page on the Peninsula and went to Sequoia High School. He attended the College of San Mateo before entering the Air Force as an aviation cadet. On the same day in December 1953 that he earned his wings and embarked on an Air Force career, he married Lou Allen Leusley, his high school classmate.

After he was declared missing, Lou Page completed a degree from Mills College while raising her children. Son Jeffrey became an electronics engineer, daughter Julie closed in on a teaching credential and son Chip worked as a freelance photographer.

She never remarried, or dated seriously. In 1996, she discovered Paradise, she said, and now works as a 64-year-old part-time proofreader for the Paradise Post.

Facing reality

Although over the years all signs pointed to her husband's death, "I never really knew what happened and there were all kinds of possibilities. After not knowing for certain, now the reality is a bit of a problem," she said.

Time is one. "He's still 33," she told the Post. "I'm not.

"The past just gets dimmer and you just sort of have to go on. The most overwhelming feeling I have is sadness — a waste of a young life with promise. I'm sad for the things he missed."

When the honor guard from Beale Air Force Base presents Mrs. Page the American flag Friday and the bugler plays taps, her children and grandchildren, family members and relatives of other missing Vietnam veterans will join her at the gravesite.

His Silver Star, the third highest honor for valor; his Air Medal, Purple Heart, Air Force Commendation Medal, Good Conduct Medal and others will be noted.

"It's just a comfort to know he's not in a box in Hawaii or someone's back yard in North Vietnam," Lou Page told the Post. "Finally he'll be buried honorably."

APRIL 1975 - OPERATION NEW LIFE

By Jacqueline Berzins
Santa Margarita Chapter, NSDAR
Oceanside, California

As a college student in the early 1960's, I became more and more aware of the problems brewing about Vietnam. My friends and classmates began to take stances on the United States' involvement in Vietnam. Some of my high school classmates even moved to Canada to avoid military service and duty in Vietnam. By my senior year in college, I was dating a young Naval ROTC officer and realized that Vietnam would be a part of my future.

In 1966, I married my ROTC officer who was, by then, an ensign in the United States Navy. Vietnam did become an integral part of our lives for the next ten years. My husband's job as a supply officer kept him busy feeding and paying military personnel and equiping ships for both the Navy and the Marines. His supply duties took us to Supply School in Athens, Georgia; the USS *Northampton*, Norfolk, Virginia; the Naval Shipyard, Boston, Massachusetts; and Sea Command, Washington, D.C.

In 1972, we were assigned to the 30th Naval Construction Regiment based on Okinawa, Japan. The regiment was comprised of several "Seabee" battalions. In 1972, the Seabees were building facilities for the Marines in Vietnam, Laos and Cambodia. My husband's job was to keep the Seabees supplied at all times.

In early 1973, as Okinawa was reverting back to Japan, my husband's command was relocated to the Naval Station at Guam. The unit's mission was still to build housing, air strips, mess halls, sanitary facilities, and other structures for troops stationed in Vietnam, the Philippines, and surrounding areas. We were living at the Naval Station, Guam, when Saigon fell to the North Vietnamese. On April 23, 1975, the United States began airlifting United States and Vietnamese personnel out of Vietnam. The Seabees were charged with the overwhelming task of converting Orote Point, an abandoned, overgrown airstrip last used in

WWII, into a tent city large enough to house thousands of Vietnam evacuees.

All the wives were asked to volunteer in support of the effort in any way we could. At first, there was nothing but chaos and confusion as no one was really in charge, and no one really knew what to do or what needed to be done. However, as busload after busload of very frightened and distraught people began to arrive, it became clear that what they needed were friendly, kind faces to welcome them and help alleviate their fears. Babies were arriving without parents or other family members. They needed hugs and smiles to calm and reassure them. Although some of the evacuees spoke English, most did not. Verbal communication was minimal.

The wives were quick to organize and facilitate care of the evacuees. The early flights were filled with mostly wealthier Vietnamese, United States Government workers, women and children. Most of the evacuees on later flights arrived without clothing, money, or identification papers. Many left Saigon with just what they had on their backs.

So many children came without family as desparate parents tossed their children onto the taxiing planes headed out of Saigon. We knew that they hoped for the best for their children and that they gave them up, knowing they might never see them again. Some of the children's parents eventually made it out on the later flights, as the flights continued nonstop for days until over 50,000 people were evacuated out of Vietnam. Later estimates elevated numbers to over 100,000 evacuees to Guam, an island where the total population was barely 80,000!

My mission was to reunite separated families. Names were gathered, but it was not an easy task as their naming customs are totally different from ours. Last names were first (sometimes), sometimes first and last names were the same, and so many had the same family name ("Ng," for example). Spelling the names was difficult since we did not speak their language, and they did not know English. We did the best we could. Lists of names were posted at a central tent in the "city." We checked constantly as new flights arrived hourly.

It was pure elation when children, parents and/or family members were reunited.

The first planes filled with wealthier Vietnamese and those who had worked for the United States Government. They arrived with luggage and money. Many tried to use their money, position, or jewelry to get better accommodations and faster processing. They soon learned that all would be treated the same regardless of their previous status in Vietnam.

The vast numbers of evacuees soon overwhelmed the tent city and its facilities. Sanitary facilities had to be burned to avoid illness; feeding the masses was a constant, ongoing operation. Lining up to wait for everything was a new concept that had to be taught. The constant rain (Guam is a tropical island) created nightmare conditions in the newly graded soil. The tents leaked, the bathing facilities were minimal, and the food was not what they were used to. Consequently, the evacuees were unhappy and uncomfortable. Their days were endless, and they were fearful of what the future had in store for them. We tried to cheer them up as best we could.

In July 1975, a new assignment beckoned us to the Naval Post Graduate School in Monterey, California - away from the Vietnamese tent city and our beautiful island of Guam. The experience with the Vietnamese people will forever have a hold on my heart. I will always remember their fortitude and determination. Years after my husband retired from the Navy and we were living in Huntington Beach, California, I learned from a client of mine that she and her family had been Vietnamese evacuees on Guam during the time we were stationed there. Thay lived in the tent city and greatly appreciated the chance the United States gave them to survive and to live and prosper in this country.

Cancelled letter from Orote Point, Guam, dated October 16, 1980.

Tent city at Orote Point, Guam.

WHAT IT TAKES TO BE A SOLDIER

By Francis Spears Bock
El Redondo Chapter, NSDAR
Redondo Beach, California

While I naively focused on my education and marriage, events during the eleven years of the Vietnam War affected my life in subtle ways. The mandatory draft, with its Selective Service registration at age eighteen was ever present on everyone's mind, especially with the escalating military action in Vietnam.

Francis Spears Bock
Eastern Hills High School JROTC
Fort Worth, Texas

In 1963 when I joined the Junior Reserve Officer's Training Corps (JROTC) as a junior at Eastern Hills High School, Fort Worth, Texas, I thought the program of classes, competitions and activities sounded interesting, patriotic, and fun. Girls were called "Sponsors" back then. The boy-girl ratio was certainly in my favor. Attending the military balls with stage band music, formal attire, and military regalia was an extra highlight for a teenage girl beginning to feel grown up.

I was proud of my father's WWII service in the Army Air Corps in England and France, and grateful that he had survived the Battles of Normandy and the Bulge. Carswell Air Force Base was nearby. The evening news about Vietnam, my American history lessons and JROTC training ignited flames of patriotic exuberance that illuminated my teenage view of the world. It enhanced my understanding of America's influence in ways that still continues to affect my attitude and patriotism.

My two years in JROTC taught me how to be self-disciplined, how to march in formation, how to shoot a rifle, how to cheer for the JROTC basketball team, how to stay warm while marching on the field in a skirt, and appreciation for the courage it takes to be a soldier. I didn't mind that my Army-green uniform required wearing my skirt below my knees. In the 1960's, wearing pants in school was not an option for girls, with the exception of the rifle range during practice and competition. The sharp-shooter award medals that I wore proudly on my uniform reinforced a self-confidence and awareness of the importance of my contribution to the team.

JROTC barracks with classrooms and a rifle range provided specialized class areas. One instructor offered unique insights into training for underwater demolitions and jungle warfare. In addition to the regular school curriculum, we had after-school and weekend practices and competitions. Under the experienced leadership of the Army instructors, JROTC students earned high achievements: All-city Brigade Commander; a championship JROTC basketball team that was undefeated for two years; highest city rating of all high school JROTC programs in the Annual Federal Inspection of 1965. The yearbook reported, "The battalion was especially commended for its fine esprit d'corps, the appearance of all uniforms, and for its ability to parade." The outstanding training prepared many students to attend college. At that time, college attendance delayed mandatory active service and offered opportunities to qualify for military jobs in other geographical areas less dangerous than Vietnam.

From my high school graduating class of 450, at least fifty-three students joined the military. Most served in Vietnam on the USS *Frank E. Evans* (DD-754) and USS *Hassayampa* (AO-145); and in places like Tuy Hoa, Da Nang, Hue, Chu Lai, and Quang Tri. Quang Tri was the most tragic because one of our graduates, a corporal and rifleman in the United States Marine Corps, was killed in action there, April, 1968, less than three years after leaving high school. The fifty-two other students returned home. One of those returning soldiers from my high school battalion expressed his opinion about his Vietnam experience for the twentieth reunion book. When asked about where he had lived, he wrote: "North Dakota, Louisiana, Guam, Taiwan, Vietnam (if that's called living)."

During my college years at North Texas State University, I was often reminded of the Vietnam War as I dodged anti-war demonstrators on the Student Union steps. During the same week, one month after my husband's graduation and our summer wedding, my husband received both his Army draft notice and his Air Force acceptance letter into Officer Training School at Lackland Air Force Base, San Antonio, Texas. With his training and degree in aeronautical engineering from Massachusetts Institute of Technology, he was assigned to the Titan missile program at Little Rock Air Force Base, also known as Tactical Air Command for its C-130's. Helicopter pilots, recently home from Vietnam, transported my husband and crew to the missile sites.

The intensified unpopularity of the war, emotional anti-war demonstrations and increased numbers of deaths and serious injuries fueled public fear and anger. Despite my cousin's outstanding airmanship and courage as a pilot on important and hazardous missions in Southeast Asia, 1969; despite the presentation of an Air Medal at Binh Thuy Air Base, Vietnam; and, despite his return home to become a Tulsa policeman, this Air Force first Lieutenant experienced more criticism than praise for his service because of the unpopularity of the war.

By 1974, mandatory draft was replaced by volunteers. Except for the soldiers who continued to serve in the Army Reserves, my classmates left the military and returned to civilian life. Reflecting on the eleven years of the Vietnam War, I appreciate my good fortune. I was able to focus on my education and marriage during a time when fear, turbulence, violence, separation, despair, and danger shared space in the hearts and minds of American citizens with security, calm, peacefulness, unification, hope, and safety. Over fifty years later, I continue to benefit from what I experienced in my high school JROTC program and to discover new ways to appreciate the courage it takes to be a soldier.

"SURE, WHY NOT?"

By Regina Rougeot Bonds
El Paso de Robles Chapter, NSDAR
Paso Robles, California

I graduated from Paso Robles High School in 1965, and I did not serve during the Vietnam War. Several of my fellow classmates dated soldiers who were stationed at Camp Roberts, north of Paso Robles. My sister, three years younger than me, dated boys from Camp Roberts and had a group of military police officers out to the house on several occasions for visits or dinner. She kept trying to set me up with dates.

I made a vow not to date soldiers. Some of the girls I graduated with married military men from Camp Roberts, and I did not like how they were treated. They got married, went back east to their husbands' home states, became pregnant and were abandoned when the men decided they didn't want to be married. I had a couple of girlfriends who married soldiers and became pregnant. Their husbands received orders to ship out to Vietnam, and when they came back home, they were not the same people. The Vietnam War did a lot of damage to our soldiers. Veterans who returned would not talk about what happened over there. Many had really bad nightmares. It was not a good situation for lasting relationships.

Despite all this, I went on a blind date with a soldier from Virginia who was in the same platoon as the military police officers, but who was never in our to the home. After the first date, I figured I was rid of him. What normal young man would want to date a girl who drove a Dodge 440 (he was a Ford man), and who went deer hunting with her cousins on her grandmother's ranch the day after the date?

A week later during the San Luis Obispo County Fair, I was asked to double date again. Having forgotten about that young soldier, I said, "Sure, why not?" We were walking to the cattle barns at the fair, and we ran into two military police from Camp Roberts. The one I was supposed to date turned out to be the same guy I had been obnoxious to the week before. We started dating. After two weeks,

Kelley Bonds asked me to marry him. I said, "Sure, why not!"

We were married a year later after Kelley was discharged from the United States Army. He was stationed at the Presideo in San Francisco and was on special assignment at Camp Roberts because of the National Guard. His duties in San Francisco were to guard military personnel who had been thrown in the brig and sent home from Vietnam, and to participate in Honor Guard duty for the funerals of the many service men killed in action. He performed military honors for as many as six funerals a day. Even now, he will not attend a funeral unless he absolutely has to.

Kelley and Regina Bonds
on their wedding day,
August 12, 1968.

During the Vietnam War, I was lucky to lose only one classmate, as well as a cousin who was in the Marines. My cousin, Ronnie, lied about his age and was sent to Vietnam. He was over there about three months when they found out he was underage. They sent him back to the states. In May 1968, when he turned 18, they sent him back to Vietnam. We got word around August 7th that he had been killed in action.

A friend, Kenny, and I had been in school together since the 7th grade. I remember coming home from San Francisco after finding out about Kenny's death and talking to his brother, Phil. Phil was determined to go over and avenge his brother's death. I talked with him about that for a long time, trying to convince him that Kenny would not want him to go to Vietnam. I asked, "If something happened to you, who would your parents have left to take care of them?"

Kelley Bonds,
United States Army Military Police

The military men and women returning from Vietnam were treated like outcasts in our own society. Their treatment was very different from what WWII veterans experienced, or what the veterans today are experiencing. After Vietnam, we didn't hear about post traumatic stress disorder (PTSD) or other psychological disorders that are diagnosed now. There were no services to help returning veterans back then. Vietnam was, and still is, a war that shouldn't have happened. You can be sure that Vietnam veterans have all of those problems and are still trying to cope with them.

My husband, Kelley, was an SP4 in the United States Army Military Police. He organized the Investigation Department at Radford University, Radford, Virginia. He retired from that department in 2001 as its deputy chief and head investigator.

THE DEAD PILE

By Diana Brenna
El Paso de Robles Chapter, NSDAR
Paso Robles, California

When I was born, my father was away serving with the Army during WWII. He didn't see me until I was seventeen months old. Being an army family, we moved a lot, but that made us more adjustable. In 1966, my cousin Ronald Sutton (captain, United States Marine Corps), went to Vietnam to serve his country. That year, my brother Philip Godwin (lance corporal, United States Marine Corps), also went to serve in Vietnam. Because both my only brother and one of my favorite cousins were serving in Vietnam, I had a lot of fear for my loved ones.

My father was horrified about my brother joining the Marines. He tried to talk him out of it by saying that the battlefield graveyards were full of heroic Marines. However, my brother wanted the challenge the toughest branch of the military offered and joined anyway. When Phil went to basic training camp at Camp Pendleton in San Diego, he was so tall (6'6") that they tried to put him in the platoon of "under achievers." He would have none of it and demanded that he be tested in sit-ups and pull-ups, or whatever, to see if he could "cut the mustard." He succeeded quite well.

In 1967, we heard from my uncle that my cousin was missing. This was quite traumatic for our entire family, and for a long time we didn't hear further news. Then we found out that my cousin had been loading his men onto a helicopter when a mortar landed nearby. He was badly wounded, thought dead, and thrown onto the "dead pile." The only reason he was saved was that his best friend saw him there and got him to a hospital. My uncle picked shrapnel out of his head and back for years afterward. Our fears for my brother escalated after getting this news. My cousin had wanted to be a career Marine officer. Since he had to be medically discharged, his hopes of a military career were at an end.

In 1968, I was getting married, and I missed my brother's support.

He was still in Vietnam. Also at this time, our country was in great upheaval with demonstrations against the war. There were harsh feelings against what our government was doing in Vietnam, a war to which President John F. Kennedy had committed us. Since I was the daughter of a military man, I had very conflicted feelings about all that was going on. On the one hand, I sympathized with the demonstrators in that I didn't want my cousin and brother to be killed in this undeclared war. Why were we involved? On the other hand, I had strong feelings as someone in a long line of family that supported our country and wanted to help where we could. It was a difficult time emotionally for our country and for me personally.

Thankfully, my brother, who served two tours in Vietnam, came home safely, only to find a country full of people who spit on their veterans, demonstrated against them, and called them "baby killers!" This came as a big shock to those idealistic young boys who were serving their country. I was so happy to see my brother come home safely. Of course, I noticed a big difference from the happy-go-lucky boy he had been. Now, he was rather quiet and withdrawn. He never talked about his service. After this, I felt bitter about the so-called "hippies" and demonstrators. I felt that the

Phil Godwin,
United States Marine Corps

sometimes violent ways in which they were expressing their views against the war and our military personnel were damaging the country and pitting Americans against one another.

In retrospect I question, "Was it worth it?" What did it gain...all those young men who sacrificed their lives, forever changing their families with the loss? I think it damaged this country badly, and we are still dealing with the Vietnam war. My brother, who is sixty-seven now, has just been diagnosed with post traumatic stress disorder. He held everything in all these years and can no longer cope with the stress by himself. He is getting help from the Veterans Administration as well as from other veteran friends. I did ask him to write for this project and he did so, as did my cousin. I think writing down a little bit of what happened helped them in some way.

I believe going to war should be a last resort after all avenues have been explored. However, once the decision to go to war is made, our outstanding military should be allowed to use all that is at its disposal to accomplish two goals: 1) to win, and 2) to convince any enemy that it would be a grave mistake to go to war with the United States of America.

Marine Home on Leave

Returning to Vietnam

Cpl. Philip W. Godwin

U.S. Marine Cpl. Philip W. Godwin has returned to Vietnam after spending a month at home on the Peninsula.

The 20-year-old son of Mr. and Mrs. William D. Godwin of Pebble Beach, Godwin volunteered to return to Vietnam though he has been serving there since April 10, 1967.

First thing his Peninsula friends noticed about Godwin was how thin he looked. He stands 6 feet 5½ inches and was down to 170 pounds, having lost 20 pounds in Vietnam. "It is so hot over there, you sweat it off," he said.

Quite Enough

The young corporal frankly said 12 months in Vietnam is quite enough for him, but he chose to extend for six months rather than risk being sent back later for another 13-month tour.

"The way I look at it, we shouldn't have gone over there in the first place, but we can't leave now. And you would be surprised how we are helping people over there through our big civic action program," Godwin said.

A 1965 graduate of Monterey High School, Godwin hopes to pursue college studies in the field of architecture following completion of his four-year hitch in 22 months.

Volunteered

He volunteered for the Marine Corps. "I guess I'd seen too many movies," he said. Upon completing basic training at the Marine Corps Recruiting Depot in San Diego, he entered radio operator school there.

That has been his job in Vietnam where he now is watch chief at the 1st Marine Air Wing Communications Center in Da Nang.

Another reason for extending, Godwin said, is the overseas savings program. He has been putting most of his pay in savings, earning 10 per cent interest under a U.S. program which offers the high interest rate as an incentive to save and thereby reduce the dollar drain.

Asked to explain how U.S. forces are helping the people over there through the civic action program, Godwin said that for a time he was a member of a medical civic action patrol.

Treat Sick

"We would go out to remote villages and treat the sick. Once the people get to know you, it is all right. But many are afraid of us and hate us," he said.

Asked if the picketing protestors of the war bothered him, Godwin said: "They have a right to express their opinion, but I think they do not realize that if they were not living in the U.S., they could be shot for what they are doing. I think they take their liberty for granted."

Godwin said Da Nang has undergone numerous rocket attacks since he has been stationed there. As for the future of the war, he said that is anyone's guess.

"What has happened with this slack of bombing of the North has pretty well confirmed my opinion and that of a lot of other guys there. Stopping the bombing didn't help end the war. It just gave them time to rest to build up another big offensive."

Article published about
Corporal Philip W. Godwin
United States Marine Corps,
page five of the
Monterey Peninsula Herald,
Monterey, California
Wednesday, July 17, 1968.

SPRING, 1962

By Susan Brooking
Gold Trail Chapter, NSDAR
Roseville, California

At the beginning of the United States involvement in Vietnam, the war didn't directly impact my daily life in any significant way. Timing is crucial. I'm of the pre-baby boomer generation. College was behind me, and the political involvement on campuses over the Vietnam War was not yet something that piqued my interest.

My generation slipped between the big wars of the 20th century. I was too young to remember many details of WWII. My only memory of that time is how handsome my uncles looked in uniform and the stories they whispered so as to not frighten the children. As an adolescent during the Korean War, my memory is of current events in social studies classes and dinner table discussions of evening news reports. Today, I realize how protected I was and just what a young adult of the 1950's I truly was.

Although I may not have been personally affected by the Vietnam War, I knew it would impact my life and our larger culture. There is a vivid touchstone event in my memory that introduced me to the Vietnam era.

It was during spring 1962 when the word, "Vietnam," first came into my consciousness. As a young United Airlines stewardess - yes, we used the word, "stewardess," in those days - although I traveled back and forth across our country, world events were not a priority. All that changed for me on an early morning flight from Chicago to Philadelphia. I noticed a female passenger sitting alone, looking nervous and deeply forlorn. The flight was not busy, so I had an opportunity to talk with her. She seemed to need someone to listen to her story. This was her first airplane ride, taking her to a big east coast city from a small midwestern farm community. In Philadelphia, she was to be met by an Army escort taking her to McGuire Air Force Base in New Jersey.

The purpose of her trip was to claim her son's body and take him home. Her son was a soldier and was killed in something called a "police action" in a place called Vietnam. We were both in tears before she completed her story. Her son was exactly my age.

That encounter changed me. I believe I became an adult that day. I realized how fragile my world was and how little I knew of the larger world. This was a beginning. The experience helped make me aware of world events, the consequences of our actions, and our individual responsibilities.

It is now fifty years later. We are reflecting on those troubled times, honoring those who served, and celebrating the veterans who sacrificed during that time in our nation's history. Our Gold Trail Chapter Daughters of the American Revolution has adopted a fifty-man housing unit at the Veterans Home of California in Yountville. A number of our adopted Yountville men are Vietnam War veterans as are a number of our chapter's HODARs ("Husbands of Daughters of the American Revolution"). Even more important to me, some of my fellow Gold Trail Daughters are Vietnam War veterans.

I came into this period of time as a sheltered and naive individual. The Vietnam era changed that for me and truly changed all of us who experienced that time. I am glad there is a way for me to make a difference for people who gave so much for our country. A simple "thank you" is just the beginning of my effort to help make so many lives whole again that were changed by the events of the Vietnam War.

BETHESDA, MARYLAND

By Judith Alger Brooks
Rancho Buena Vista Chapter, NSDAR
Vista, California

I served as a Navy nurse from 27 November 1965 to 30 December 1967. I was stationed at the National Naval Medical Center in Bethesda, Maryland. Those were very heavy casualty times. Most of the wounds were very silimilar to those encountered in the Iraqi and Afghanistan wounded in recent times, but also included diseases such as malaria, dysentery, and dengue fever.

Judith Alger Brooks
United States Navy Nurse Corps

I was amazed at how resilient these young men were. They believed that what they were doing was valuable and thought highly of the South Vietnamese people. I was distraught by the night terrors they displayed. I heard stories of how children were booby trapped and sent to a trooper whose instinct was to squat to hug the child or to hand out candy. By the time they returned to the United States, it was very unlikely they would die. However, there were those who did die, an occasion that was truly heartbreaking for the staff.

Our beds, and those of the Veterans Administration hospitals were so full. I remember sending a man home in a body cast to his mother, who was a nurse. She managed to get him to outpatient VA services.

The memory that still irritates me to this day is of the anti-war demonstrations in Washington, D.C. In those days, military personnel were hospitalized until they could return to active duty or until they were medically discharged. As an example, an appendectomy patient could be allowed liberty to go into town and return for the night. Even after patients were no longer required to wear uniforms off base, we had many return from liberty with injuries from being attacked by the demonstrators.

I often wonder how many of the 390,000 Vietnam War veterans who were wounded are getting any of the services that are now available?

As fate would have it, I fell in love with a Marine and got married. In those days, women couldn't be in the military if they were married or had children. So, I only served two years.

THE MILITARY BRIDE

By Janet Buckley
Josefa Higuera Livermore Chapter, NSDAR
Livermore, California

I was a young bride of one year when Richard's squadron was sent to Vietnam. I left the Marine Corps Air Station Base at El Toro, California, and went home to stay with my parents. They had also experienced a country in conflict during WWII. I am sure they had renewed fears and stress as their daughter now lived through military action. In 1965, Vietnam was not acknowledged by the general public as a war with United States involvement, so the aircraft carriers leaving with flight squadrons aboard were leaving with little or no fanfare.

Marine Corps jet pilot Richard Buckley on his way to Vietnam.

The tensions and fears held by military families were privately expressed. Interestingly enough, amidst the secrecy, there was a photograph on the front page of the Costa Mesa newspaper the day I returned home to Livermore for a thirteen-month stay, that showed my husband's flight squadron leaving San Diego for Vietnam.

During my husband's deployment, I was able to go to Japan when the squadron was on "R & R." We had one month together in Japan and one month in Okinawa. Richard had been gone for six months by that time, and I was more than ready to brave whatever had to be endured to be with him. Once again, the details of my travel were kept secret. I was told on the way to Iwakuni, Japan - on the bullet train from Tokyo - not to mention the names of any of the men in the squadron since the group had already lost one-third of its members. This was in early 1966, and these were men and wives I knew. The awful reality of war was coming close to home.

I was in college at California State College, Hayward, during the first months of Richard's tour. I walked the campus with protestors screaming and tear gas being thrown. I couldn't imagine why our boys had no support back home. My own husband had left college and qualified as a young Marine officer and pilot. He really just wanted to fly as he had when he was a teenager. He wanted to serve his country as his brothers, had, but he didn't want war as such.

Now as a mother of three grown sons, we are both very thankful that none of them had to serve in Iraq and other areas of conflict. I now better understand the "pacifist stand" but will never get over how our men were treated upon returning to the United States.

Richard completed 121 missions - twenty-one over North Vietnam - and was a decorated pilot. He was a very young lieutenant due to losses among the older men who flew in the war. The picture shown on the next page is after his return. I am pinning his captain's bars on his uniform. Richard served another year of active military duty in the Marine Corps before Congressman Donald Edwards gave him an early release to return to college.

After his release, we lived in San Jose on a military pension for college. Both of us went back to school and finished our degrees. Yes, even then, we had to walk back and forth to San Jose State College, amid tear gas being hurled at the protestors and spitting, screaming demonstrators protesting United States involvement in the war.

Richard and I just celebrated our fiftieth wedding anniversary. Our early married years during an awful situation have probably played a big part in the way we hang in there together during trying times. We are thankful for what we have been given when so many weren't as fortunate. Richard still works in the Livermore company he founded in the 1970's. In the last ten years, he has become the founder of "Peace and Conflict Resolution," located on his website, *BuckleyRealty.com*.

Although it is late, it is interesting to see how many organizations,

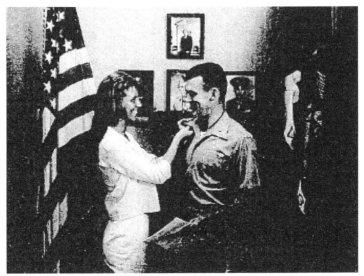

Newspaper photograph of Janet Buckley pinning Captain's bars on her husband's uniforn after his return home from a thirteen-month tour of duty in Vietnam.

including the Veterans of Foreign Wars, that at first didn't recognize Vietnam War veterans as veterans from a "real war," now honor the veterans of that conflict. Richard has two bricks that have been placed on the walk in front of the Livermore VFW Hall to honor him as a local boy who fought a fight no one really wanted but many had to endure.

Honor comes in many forms, and Richard has never sought recognition. We have a POW bracelet framed in his office that our son obtained for him when he visited the Vietnam Wall in Washington, D.C. The bracelet honors a former co-pilot who served with him who has never been found.

Richard also met a pilot in a library in the Philippines after they both ferried a vintage aircraft there for restoration. They talked about our mutual Georgia relation who, before capture, served with Senator John McCain. We saw John McCain in 1972 when he was released. Before his release, and on our return to California from our last station in North Carolina (1967), we had the privilege of taking his capture information to his family in Georgia.

Richard was a grand marshal of the Livermore Rodeo and presented a flag to the Livermore School District office soon after his home-coming.

Life has been good to us. We have gone on to raise wonderful sons. We can now reflect on a time that was not popular in our own country. Maybe that is okay. We learn, and grow, and question - and that is also okay.

"YOU JUST DO WHAT YOU GOTTA DO"

By Janet Burkett
Sierra Foothills Chapter, NSDAR
Oakhurst, California

For me, some of the most poignant memories of the Vietnam era included writing letters and waiting for responses; packing boxes of goodies with my mother to ship to loved ones; and later, at the end of the nightly newscast, watching a dark television screen with names of that day's deceased scrolling across for what seemed an eternity. Just the number of names was overwhelming. We watched and read in silence, holding our breath, hoping not to see familiar names appear and roll across the television screen. We knew full well that anything could have happened since that night's list was compiled. We were left with a partial sense of relief but also with a sense of anxiety, knowing that we would be in front of the television screen again the next evening.

Janet's brother, Tom, arriving at Da Nang, Vietnam.

It was 1969. My brother, cousin, and a best friend were all serving in Vietnam. My brother, Tom, was stationed in Da Nang and Chu Lai with a medical detachment. My cousin, Joey, was in the combat field with the 101st Airborne Division. My friend, Larry, was flying helicopters in and out of the war zone. All three were so young and preparing for bright futures that would soon be interrupted and changed forever. They were going to school, surfing, working, enjoying family and friends. They all knew that their idylic time was probably going to be cut short because of the draft. Chances were pretty good, they would be shipped off to a distant jungle from which they might not return.

Fortunately, all three of them made it back to the United States, but not without scars and haunting memories that would last for the rest of their lives.

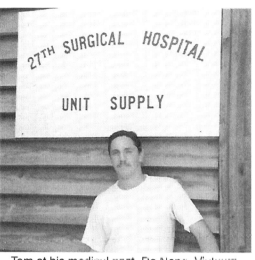

Tom at his medical post, Da Nang, Vietnam.

Enemy strike at Da Nang, April 1969.

Cousin Joey eventually died some years after the Vietnam War as a result of intense exposure to Agent Orange. Once, he wrote to me that he hadn't run into my brother, Tom, in Vietnam. He said he hoped he never did, because if he did, it would mean Tom was either in a hospital or out in the field.

Going through saved letters now, I can read about the loneliness, the longing for home and family, the countdown of days remaining in "Nam," the intense heat, the ferociousness of the enemy, and the unimaginable horrors of battle. A current expression, "You just do what you gotta do," certainly applied to the young men who were just there doing what their country asked them to do. Returning home to a country that seemed to look down on their service and on the uniform they had worn with pride had to be devastating. I don't know how to comprehend what they must have felt. I hope and pray that as a nation, we now have learned what sacrifices were made and how brave these true heroes really were.

Barracks at Da Nang, Vietnam.
Bomb shelter is in the distance on the right.

Closeup of a bomb shelter at Da Nang, Vietnam.

UNDAUNTED

By Nancy Jo Carrier
Susan B. Anthony Chapter, NSDAR
Long Beach, California

My brother and boyfriend returned from the local Army recruiter, announcing that they were joining the army on the "buddy plan." Their plan was to go through basic training and airborne school together. Departure day, December 13, 1965, was difficult knowing that Vietnam could be a destination in the near future. Separation from one another was inevitable as my boyfriend was injured during boot camp and was held back…while my brother, William B. "Bill" Haggard, continued on with his training alone.

Sergeant William B. Haggard,
Special Forces, United States Army

During WWII, our dad was stationed in the Aleutian Islands for over three years. The military formed his behavior and, being his children, ours as well. Direct eye contact, proper English, no sassing, respect for others, good posture, and no talking at the supper table were our directives. It seems apparent to me, now, that Bill and my younger brother, Jim, both of whom served in Vietnam, wanted to prove their abilities and make "Daddy" proud.

After basic training, Bill decided that he wanted to join the Army Special Forces, the elite fighting soldiers with a unique role in our military. He was sent to Fort Bragg, North Carolina, for difficult, rigorous physical fitness training and challenging courses of study designed to admit him into the brotherhood of the selectively and competitively chosen. Then, it was off to Fort Benning, Georgia, for the Army Airborne School. His choice of duty was medical and following that additional training, he graduated from the Medical Field Service School at Fort Sam Houston, Texas, January 1967. In September, Bill returned home on leave for my wedding to the boyfriend who had entered the military with him. All eyes were on Bill at Los Angeles International Airport as he sported his perfectly creased uniform, bloused pants over the spit-shined military boots...and on his head... the Army Special Forces "Green Beret." Safely wrapped in his duffle bag were his orders for Vietnam.

Specialist 4 Haggard was soon serving as senior medical advisor in Camp Dak To, located in a deep valley in the Central Highlands of Vietnam. A Viet Cong mortar attack destroyed two of three C-130 planes located on the airstrip and ignited a nearby ammunitions dump. For the next eighteen hours, unfired mortars and shrapnel bombarded the near camp. Bill was busy tending to the injured. It was reported that one massive fireball explosion left two 40-foot craters. It was thought to be one of the largest explosions, if not the largest, of the war. For the next year, *Bac-Si* (doctor) Haggard lived along side of the Montagnards, the Vietnam mountain people.

I remember our family anticipating the evening news on television. Talk of battles, mortars, the wounded and dead were often too much to bear. Some letters never came...cell phones and email had not yet been invented. I have sad memories of my mother kneeling beside her bed in prayer, softly crying as she pleaded for God to bring my brother back safely. The Vietnam War was the first to have such full media coverage. We wanted to know, but we didn't want to know. When letters came, we read and reread the words. We would start planning his return...and then the evening news was on again.

In January and February 1968, the Tet Offensive in Vietnam shook the American public to its core. The news media seemed to thrive on the aggression and horrors of the war. In addition to the pain and fears depicted in the news from Southeast Asia, there was so much civilian unrest and political upheaval occurring domestically. My parents carried heavy hearts and wore wrinkles of worry on their faces the entire year that Bill was in Vietnam.

The movie *Green Berets*, telling the story of the elite fighting force and starring John Wayne, George Takei, and David Janssen, was released in 1968. My chest seemed to swell with pride knowing that my brother was one of the best. Friends and family would call to check on my brother and our family's welfare. Mother needed all the encouragement, positive thoughts, and prayers that could be mustered. Brother Bill praised the movie, claiming it to be most realistic and true with regard to what was happening with Special Forces in Vietnam.

And then in July of 1968, we received a letter accompanied by a declaration that Sergeant William B. Haggard had received THE BRONZE STAR MEDAL WITH VALOR FOR HEROISM:

For heroism in connection with ground operations against a hostile force in the Republic of Vietnam: Sergeant Haggard distinguished himself on 17 May 1968, while serving as a medical specialist and advisor to a camp strike force platoon, engaged in the mission of providing security for a mine-sweeping operation. The platoon came under a heavy attack from a company of well entrenched enemy soldiers. Ignoring his own personal safety, he quickly organized the platoon and led an assault on the enemy force. Noticing that several wounded troops were unable to move and still lying in exposed positions a short distance from the enemy positions, Sergeant Haggard braved withering automatic weapons fire to move to the aid of the wounded time after time. After personally carrying six wounded troops to safety, he then applied his astute medical knowledge, and treated the wounded men and prepared them for evacuation. The quick reaction, expert medical treatment, and brave actions performed by Sergeant Haggard, greatly contributed toward saving the lives of six soldiers. His great concern for his fellow man, intensive dedication and heroism in action were in keeping with the highest traditions of the military service and reflect great credit upon himself, the Special Forces, and the United States Army.

Bill was also the recipient of the Purple Heart for his battle wounds. He returned from Southeast Asia later in the year, and was sent to Fort Ord, California, with what was first thought to be malaria. It was later diagnosed as Hodgkin's disease. Agent Orange, a chemical sprayed on the jungles of Vietnam to kill the growth and clear the areas for battle, was later determined to be a major cause of Hodgkin's disease. Months of cobalt treatments and radiation wore down his resistance, but he fought and continued to fight. However, ten years following his return from Vietnam, Sergeant William B. Haggard succumbed to complications of his treatment. He was thirty-two years old.

My younger brother, Jim, left for Vietnam one year after Bill's return home. Mother and Dad were facing another year of horrific newsreels and hostilities towards our military on the home front. It was most difficult. My husband at that time, having also served in Vietnam, suffered post traumatic stress that contributed to the end of our marriage. War tends to have a trickle-down effect on all connected.

Almighty God had a plan, and I try to focus on the bigger picture. Sergeant Bill Haggard made possible the lives of at least six fellow soldiers who returned to their homes and families. Hopefully, they are now fathers and the grandfathers who are looked up to and admired by their offspring.

My brother shared with my mother that he changed his underwear before heading out on patrol because, as mothers often say, "What would they think of your mother if something should happen to you. and you don't have on clean underwear?"

And yes, Daddy was proud!

DR. MARK KRUGMAN

By Sally Cicuto
Conejo Valley Chapter, NSDAR
Thousand Oaks, California

War is an assault to the senses and while it may be organized murder and mayhem there are scars that are left upon the individual who must participate and execute that war. Army Sgt. Ed Tingstrom

As a DAR Daughter, it is vitally important for me to tell the story of my brother-in-law, Dr. Mark Krugman, and how he has inspired me with his altruistic compassion. I met Mark after the Vietnam War in 1989 when he married my sister. Today, I am not only so impressed with what he accomplished during the Vietnam War, but with his continued volunteer service to our veterans. By giving of his specialized skills and talents, he promotes a true goodness so that our veterans who have suffered traumatic afflictions might feel normal again.

We all know about the sacrifices our soldiers have made to maintain our treasured freedoms. It makes sense to me that it is everyone's responsibility to care about our veterans and to do what we can with the talents we have to help improve their lives. This is the lesson I learned from my

Major Mark Krugman, MD
United States Air Force, Vietnam War Era
Offutt Air Force Base, Nebraska

brother-in-law who is the epitome of what it means to give of oneself for country. To this day, he continues his service to improve the quality of life for our wounded warriors.

Major Krugman, MD served in the Air Force during the Vietnam

War era, as a specialist in otolaryngology (ENT). He was stationed at Offutt Air Force Base in Nebraska, Headquarters of the Strategic Air Command. A four-star general, seventeen other generals and an admiral were also stationed there for national security purposes.

Otolaryngology is the medical specialty dealing with ear, nose, and throat conditions. Our Air Force pilots were plagued with ENT problems. They often suffered from persistent ear blocks, sinus pressure, tinnitus and hearing loss caused by high altitude flying, rapid changes in altitude, and decompression caused by banking the aircraft to slip in and out of enemy territory. Persistent sinusitis was deadly for a pilot. The worst condition was vertigo so severe the pilots couldn't tell if they were flying sideways, upside down or into the ground.

After his service at Offutt Air Force Base, Dr. Krugman received an outstanding commendation allowing him to choose a post anywhere in the country. Having had experience with Nebraska's harsh winters, he said, "Somewhere warm!" His next tour of duty was as assistant professor of otolaryngology at UCLA's School of Medicine. Always interested in the field of plastic surgery, he went from UCLA ENT to UCI plastic surgery where he holds Board Certifications in both specialties. While in private practice, he served on the faculty at both universities.

As a plastic surgeon, Dr. Krugman volunteered his time and surgical skills to our veterans and burn victims through the Shriner's Children's Hospital in Los Angeles. One patient, an Iraqi boy, the unfortunate victim of a land mine, inspired him to provide similar services to our wounded warriors. Now, he volunteers at the Naval Medical Center in San Diego, California, in the C.A.R.E. program (Comprehensive Advanced Restorative Effort). The C.A.R.E. program focuses on surgical, medical, and emotional support for the traumatically injured who suffer from major life-altering injuries or severe disfigurement.

My brother-in-law now lectures at the Naval Medical Center on hair restoration for burn victims. He also assists with those surgeries on veterans suffering from the effects of Improvised Explosive

Devices (IED's), ultimately helping them with their self-esteem and providing emotional support for the trauma they suffered.

Today, Dr. Krugman lives in Orange County with his wife, Dr. Jane Curtis, and daughter, Allison Krugman, a student in international relations at Claremont-McKenna College. My deepest appreciation is extended to him for his service during the Vietnam War and for his continuing devotion to our servicemen. He has made a deep impression on me and on his entire family. We are so proud of the continued service that he provides for our wounded warriors. As a DAR Daughter, and his sister-in-law, I am especially moved by the exemplary compassion he has for our veterans. He has shown me what can be done to improve their lives, using the special God-given gifts that we may have.

Mark Krugman, MD (center) with VA medical staff
Naval Medical Center, San Diego, California

THE WAR OF SHAME

By Donna Cohen
El Paso de Robles Chapter, NSDAR
Paso Robles, California

My paternal ancestors arrived in the North American colonies in the early 1600's. In every conflict, my family has fought for our country and our liberties. I was born in 1952. Many of my cousins, classmates and friends were drafted and served in the Vietnam War. When we graduated from high school in 1970, the conflict was in high gear, and every young man was afraid his "number" would be pulled in the draft lottery. In so many ways, my generation was lost during this conflict.

Everything was changing - music, television, clothing, hair, the way people spoke to each other, lack of respect for our fellow brothers and sisters, our parents - everywhere, everything was changing. I believe that the two biggest changes were: 1) constant, negative reporting, and 2) lack of respect, not just for our military personnel, but for people in general. It was the era of "Make love, not war!" and "Me, Me, Me!" We had to "feel good." Broadcast and printed news was negative and distorted, showing how awful our soldiers were. I always believed every single one who served was a hero!

I remember the worst thing my grandmother ever told me, "Every generation has a war. This one is bad. I'm ashamed our president won't let our boys win this war!" To hear that from my grandmother broke my heart. I never will forget those words. My grandmother was a Gold Star Mother whose four sons were all serving in the military at the same time. My Uncle Robert was killed on his way home during WWII. She mourned his loss every day. That's when I realized this was the "War of Shame," not because of our soldiers, but because of the politicians, newscasters and movie stars who said such horrible things about our men. There were sit–ins, marches, protests whose participants were saying our soldiers were "baby killers." These young men we sat next to in school, dated, laughed with, and even cried with – they were "baby killers?" How could this be?

My grandmother was proud and believed that the United States was the greatest country in the world. She believed in a strong and brave America, a place where anyone could be anything - freedom and liberty for all. She took the privilege of voting very seriously. Even if her candidate didn't win, he or she earned respect by virtue of running for office.

Many of our brave soldiers who fought in the Vietnam War did not enlist. They were drafted. The "Vietnam Conflict" as they called it, was so terrible because no one wanted to recognize the men and women who fought bravely, and worse, those who died. Those who went didn't choose to go to war. They were sent to war. I still see the disrespect today, and it greatly saddens me.

I remember talking to one of my uncles, my mother's brother, a veteran of both WWII and the Korean War. My uncle experienced a different side no one had ever spoken about. He was a career military man who was troubled because he retired when he received orders to report for duty in Vietnam. That revelation slipped out - he has never spoken about it since. He had never fought in a war like Vietnam. He was used to "civilized war." How can war be civilized? I believe the difference was in the propaganda fed to us by media. There are always innocents injured or killed in any war. The very nature of war is not civilized.

A friend - one of many who served, but one of the few to ever talk about his experience - told me a few of the things he had been through. There isn't enough room to write his story, but only to say, "We went in to fight, but not to win." How very sad. Our soldiers were never given the orders they needed, "Go fight, win, and come home victorious." That's why I call it a "War of Shame." Our veterans are not shameful. They are all heroes, every one of them. To all the men and women who have served our country in any war, but especially to those who served in the Vietnam War and who have not properly felt or known our expressed heartfelt appreciation, "Thank you for your service to our country!"

MICHAEL'S STORY

By Jane Coté
Josefa Higuera Livermore Chapter, NSDAR
Livermore, California

My story is one of ultimate friendship and sacrifice, one which fills my heart with pride for having know such a man. I have tears of sadness for he has since passed. There are such special memories of an amazingly selfless man who I had the privilege of calling my friend - Michael Phillip McCauley, EM1, United States Coast Guard.

The United States Coast Guard is not usually included when the Armed Forces are mentioned. The Coast Guard falls under the jurisdiction of the Department of Homeland Security. However, the men of the USCG have served our country since 1790 and fought in every war since the War of 1812. Throughout the Vietnam War, some 8,000 Coast Guard personnel served on the rivers and the coastline of Vietnam alongside the United States Navy. In 1965, my husband, Bernard Robert Coté, FM1, USCG, was stationed in Boston where he met and became fast friends with Michael, a soft-spoken, caring man, who soon became a part of our family.

Bernard Coté and his friend, Michael McCauley

Bernard and I married in 1966 and, in March of 1967, became parents of our precious daughter, Christine. Soon after, in June, Bernard received orders for Vietnam. I was devastated and terrified as I had already lost two dear friends to the war, each at the age of 19, the same age as we were. I couldn't begin to imagine losing my husband, whom I had known since the age of six, or the thought of our daughter never knowing her daddy. But I soon learned that, unlike other branches of the military, the Coast Guard had a policy that, with approval of the base commanding officer, a sailor could volunteer to serve another's tour of duty. This is what Michael unselfishly did for us. Still today, some 48 years later, I become choked up when I remember Michael giving me a hug and telling me not to worry, that he would make sure that my husband and daughter would stay safe. He kept his word.

Thankfully, Mike came home to us safely after serving that year of duty. We were so very blessed to have had him in our lives for thirty years. Sadly, we lost him in 1995. He may be gone from the physical world, but he will live on forever in a special place in our hearts.

FREDERICK HOWARD HENDERSON

By Muriel Henderson Crawford
Anne Loucks Chapter, NSDAR
Martinez, California

When the Vietnam War began, I was a mother of two little girls with a third to follow in the next few years. My husband, Barry, and I lived in a small house in Berkeley, California. A family with a teen-aged daughter and a son in his early twenties lived in the house next door. This was a friendly and helpful family. I sometimes asked Harriett, the mother, for advice, and often relied on the daughter for babysitting. Their last name was Henderson, the same as my maiden name, and we wondered if we were distantly related.

Muriel Crawford and her three daughters, 1965
Berkeley, California

Barry worked during the day, leaving me alone with the children. One afternoon, I heard strange noises in my house. I began calling for help. Our neighbors' son, who was on leave from West Point, heard my cries and immediately came to my "rescue." There was no intruder in the house, but I appreciated his kindness and bravery. His name was Frederick Howard Henderson.

Berkeley was a liberal place, as it still is. We knew people who said that young men should resist the draft, burn their draft cards, and escape to Canada. I disagreed and was shocked that people would blame young men who obeyed the law and went into the military when they were drafted. I remember thinking, "Well, I'm glad I have daughters." However, I worried about the young men who were in harm's way, and I wished that we had never entered the war. Barry and I sometimes argued about it. He thought the government knew what it was doing. I wasn't so sure.

Our neighbor, Fred Henderson, wasn't drafted. He had long been determined to serve his country. His West Point classmates noted the following:

Captain Frederick Howard Henderson
United States Army

Undoubtedly influenced by his father's patriotic service in two wars, Fred's lifelong dream was to attend West Point and make the U.S. Army his career. After graduation from high school, Fred attended the University of California at Berkeley from 1956 to 1959 while making repeated attempts to secure a nomination to West Point... Nothing shows how determined he was to get into West Point more than his willingness to start his college career over again at West Point after spending three years at the University of California... Fred deployed to Vietnam with his unit most likely in the early part of 1966. [Captain Frederic Howard Henderson's] final battle - Operation Attleboro - one of the largest operations of the Vietnam War, commenced in early November 1966. Fred led his unit, C Company, in an air assault to rescue B Company which had been cut off by enemy forces in the woods near the landing zone. Unfortunately, the landing zone was surrounded by a large and well dug-in enemy force. Fred was killed leading the company in the assault and his company took about 50 percent casualties. Fred led from the front and his Silver Star citation attests to his bravery and the loyalty he felt toward his men for which he died in battle.

Barry and I will never forget hearing Fred's mother scream. When I heard that scream I knew without being told what had happened. Harriet was not an excitable woman, but she screamed over and over when she got the news that her son had been killed in Vietnam. She could not be consoled. What can you say to a mother who loses her only son?

Barry and I had had our third daughter in 1965. We had outgrown our small house, and shortly after Fred's death we moved to a larger house a few miles away in Lafayette, California. In 1971, we moved to Illinois. We were a busy young family, and we lost touch with our Berkeley neighbors.

In the 1980's, Barry and I visited Washington, D.C. "Let's go look at the Vietnam Veterans' Memorial," I suggested. So we went to the wall with all the names of those who had died in the Vietnam War. However, for some reason I have never understood, and although we looked diligently, we could not find the name of our young neighbor who died in the war. It's there: "Frederick Howard Henderson, Panel 12E, Row 14." I'm determined to see it the next time I'm in Washington, D.C.

"SO, YOU WANT ME TO WRITE!"

By Marian Wright DeMars
Sierra Amador Chapter, NSDAR
Jackson, California

So you want us to write memoirs of the Vietnam War, and you try to convince me that it happened fifty years ago. Well, I'm not buying it. It was yesterday that my sons were teenagers with draft numbers, and I was a wreck. I paced my kitchen night after night.

My family members fought in every war this country has ever had: King Phillip's, Queen Anne's, the Revolution, the War of 1812, the Civil War on both sides, World War II and Korea. My mother said that we had a soldier in World War I. I have not found him. However, Vietnam was an undeclared war. We had not been attacked, and my sons were my life.

I reacted badly in front of my DAR chapter sisters when this theme was announced. So I had to go home and have a talk with myself. I never watched the constant television news or the movies about the Vietnam War; and obviously, I have never come to grips with the Vietnam War. The draft ended just above my oldest son's lottery number, and he doesn't even remember that.

I have missed several good movies and television shows because I will never support Jane Fonda. She remains a traitor in my eyes. Other traitors to our country have gone to jail. She has just continued to have a life. When my husband, a Korean War veteran, had to go into the Los Angeles VA hospital for treatment of a wound that never healed, hundreds of cars in the parking lot bore bumper stickers calling Jane Fonda a traitor. This was years after the Vietnam War, but the veterans have not forgotten.

Then my brain kicked in, and I realized that this memoir is not supposed to be about me, but rather about a young man who became a friend of my husband. My husband and I ran our own business. When we were close to selling it and retiring, my husband began going uptown for afternoon coffee with a group of men. There he met the man who is my example.

I wish I could recall this man's name, but he is probably representative of many. He joined the military when he was eighteen years old. Shortly afterward, he found himself in the jungle and alone. He had become separated from his unit. He was being shot at and admitted to being scared to death. When he got home again, he flew to New York City. He caught a taxi and the driver asked him where he was coming from. The young man said "Vietnam," and the driver never spoke another word to him.

When my husband met him, this young man was living in a warehouse in town. He was a night watchman and an artist. We went to his warehouse/studio, and he gave me a beautiful painting of a herd of horses on a green field. I eventually gave the painting to my son, but I made him listen to the artist's story first. The artist had found himself unable to merge back into "regular" life.

I am not sure if the American Legion and the Veterans of Foreign Wars tried to tell us to be compassionate, or if they dropped the ball on this duty. I know that I never thought beyond my two sons, believing that they would be compassionate if I told them to. However, this memoir project is not about me or my sons, but about that artist and so many others who were conflicted, but served anyway.

Because jungle fighting and chemical weapons are different from other warefare, and because war is hell, many still suffer from ailments. There must be heroes out there who still suffer from our response to their service, and that is not OK. I apologize to them.

FLYING THE FRIENDLY SKIES"

By Louise Diracles
Acalanes Chapter, NSDAR
Lafayette, California

I was a Pan American Airways stewardess from 1967-1973. I flew military personnel for rest and recreation in and out of Saigon, Cam Rahn Bay, and Da Nang, Vietnam. I would always ask to sit in the cockpit on landing, frequently at night. I could see mortars going off like fireworks. It was a frightening time. Pan Am planes often had bullet holes in them. You had to volunteer for these flights. Pan Am stewardesses got prisoner of war cards in case we were captured.

Stewardesses flew the military personnel to their two-week rest and recreation vacations in places like Australia, Hawaii, and Guam. It was so much fun going out of Vietnam; it was always a party. The guys were the best passengers ever. We'd get on the loud speaker and say, "Boys, it would really help us if you could crush your milk cartons so we could stow the trays more easily." You should have heard the bang, bang, bang of those milk cartons being smashed!

Pan American Airlines Stewardess
Louise Diracles

On the return trips back into Vietnam, the mood was somber. One soldier gave me his stuffed kangaroo. I tried to refuse, but he said it would just get moldy in his locker. I treasure that gift and wonder if that soldier made it back to the United States.

Although I didn't participate in the evacuation of Saigon after the fall of Vietnam, my colleagues talked about it. They said there were people holding up their babies over the fence, begging the stewardesses to take them on the plane. There were many more babies than the plane could hold. Babies were put in the overhead compartments for take-off and landing. Babies were strapped to the stewardesses. The local money (piasters) was collected in pillow cases and given to men with machine guns on the tarmac, who then let more people on the plane. It was the most terrifying, and yet the most gratifying, time.

My husband, Kramer Klabau, was in the Vietnam War. He was in his senior year at the University of Oregon, draft number 123. He took the Navy officer's test and was sent to Newport, Rhode Island, June 1968. He volunteered for the Navy's Underwater Demolition Team (UDT) and passed all the physical and mental requirements, but the Navy had reached its quota and his class was passed over. While attending another naval school, he met a fellow officer who was two classes behind him and who had completed his UDT training. He told Kramer that he enjoyed the training, but he was being advanced to SEAL training, which he knew little about.

Kramer was then assigned to the ammunition ship USS *Mauna Kea* (AE-22), based at Concord Naval Weapons Station in Concord, California. There were 13 officers and 230 enlisted men assigned to the *Mauna Kea*. The ship's mission was to pass ammunition in the form of bombs and shells to aircraft carriers, cruisers, and destroyers in the South China Sea off the coast of Vietnam. The ship would spend a few days replenishing supplies at Subic Bay Naval Station in the Philippines before going out on 30-day deployments to pass cargo via cables to the ships stationed off the Vietnam coast.

The *Mauna Kea* received a commendation medal for assisting the rescue of a civilian freighter caught in a powerful typhoon. During the typhoon the cannon barrels on the ship were bent by the power of the sea.

Kramer asks us to remember all the soldiers who are currently serving in today's non-draft military, as well as the veterans from Vietnam and other wars.

A LETTER FROM ALLEN

By Katharine Dixon, MD
De Anza Chapter, NSDAR
Encinitas, California

Going through my mother's letters in 2011, I came across a letter written to her from Staff Sergeant Allen Dillow who was with the Air Force 14th Special Operations Wing. Allen Dillow was my mother's nephew and my cousin. We were about the same age and both children of clannish Appalachia. I always joked about having a crush on him when we were young, so handsome was he in his uniform.

Sergeant Dillow served four years in Vietnam, from 1965 to 1969. He wrote to my mother from Nha Trang, Vietnam (February 9, 1966) as follows:

Dear Aunt Ramona and Girls,
I would like to express my sincere thanks for your thoughtfulness at Christmas time, a card, note, or just about anything is appreciated over here. We service men are not robots taught to kill. We still have a heart, and like to be thought of at such times. We are over here halfway around the world, in a hostile land, not only a foreign land, away from our loved ones. Where everyday things seem as such to you, they would be like a gift from heaven to us. Hot water, cold glass of milk, cold can of beer, seeing friendly eyes, someone that you could reach out and touch, or maybe even kiss, that are only gleams in our eyes that we have to wait a year for. But being what it is, and being the kind of men we are "supposed" to be, we must never complain, even though at nights you still hear sniffles from these men, not excluding me.
I don't hear much from home but I do hope things have worked out for the best. Daddy is the greatest as far as I am concerned. He has his faults, but we all do, none of us are perfect. If we were we would not be on this earth.
Do tell grandmother I said hello and hope this finds her in good health.
Tell Ray [my brother who was in the Ohio National Guard] that if it is at all possible not to get messed up with this over here. May he

64

stay home as long as possible, and for God's sake don't volunteer, don't get star struck by some John Wayne type movie, it isn't fought that way. Do take care, and thank you again for your kind and warm thoughts.
Allen

While Allen was in Vietnam, I finished medical school at Ohio State University. All but seven women and two conscientious objectors from our 1967 graduating class of 150 students went into the military under the Berry Plan, or "doctor draft," including my husband.

Many of these students, my friends, served in Vietnam. The two conscientious objectors were required to spend two years with the United States Public Health Service or Indian Health as an alternative to the draft.

After leaving Vietnam, Allen served another eighteen years in the Air Force, mostly overseas. Our clan is so proud of him and his service.

Staff Sergeant Allen Dillow
United States Air Force

MY BROTHER, ROBERT J. MᶜCULLOUGH, JR.

By Carol Driesen
El Palo Alto Chapter, NSDAR
Palo Alto, California

In 1965, rather than face the draft, my brother, Robert J. McCullough, Jr., joined the Air Force. He became a navigator. On December 24, 1966, he traveled from Tacoma, Washington, to Vietnam on a contract airliner. He was not happy to be heading out on Christmas Eve. Even worse, when he landed in Japan, it was already December 26th. He completely missed Christmas that year. After a couple of days getting settled in Taiwan, his actual base, he made his first visit to Vietnam. At one of the first bases where his plane landed, the American artillery was firing shells down the runway at some target. The sound of shelling was something he heard frequently for the next six years.

Since American planes were fairly large, they were called "mortar magnets." The Viet Cong were especially eager to destroy as many C-130 transports as possible. So the Army or Marine troops on the ground liked to get them off their runways as soon as possible.

Many dead or wounded soldiers were brought back from forward locations. Once, my brother's crew brought eleven dead South Vietnamese soldiers back to their hometown. Family members were traveling with the bodies. As the plane climbed up to altitude, the bodies, which had been out in the sun for several days, began to rupture. The stench was unbearable and the family members were scrambling in the back of the aircraft to try to escape

Captain Robert J. McCullough, Jr.
United States Air Force

that smell. Every possible hatch was opened, and the pilots got the aircraft down to the ground as soon as possible.

It was an especially cruel experience for those poor family members.

My brother recalls that many of our aircraft were transporting essential combat supplies to an airfield somewhere in the "boonies," several times a day, three days in a row, followed by a day off. When they landed, there would often be bullet holes in the aircraft, but usually nothing too serious. However, one of his buddies' aircraft was going in to that same field, and it was hit by ground fire. Unfortunately, the plane was carrying a load of shells and fuses which blew up when hit by a round from the ground. All on board were killed.

Sometimes the crews had to fly along the Vietnam-Laos border for thirteen hours while the radio operators in the back of the aircraft provided command and control to fighters, bombers, and other operations. While the flights were boring, they gave good radio communication for all kinds of combat activities going on throughout the region. The old saying, "Flying is hours and hours of sheer boredom interrupted by moments of stark terror," has a ring of truth.

One day, they were assigned to pick up some Army equipment at Dalat, an airfield in the mountains at over 4,900 feet altitude. The load turned out to be an asphalt-spreader truck. As was his practice, the loadmaster computed his figures, based on what the Army told him about the weight of the truck. As they rolled down the runway for takeoff, the plane felt very sluggish, but they were soon at the point of no return. The entire crew was tense as the end of the runway came up and the pilot hauled back on the yoke. The plane staggered into the air, with the crew not sure they would keep flying. Thankfully they did, and back at the base they found that the Army had neglected to tell them that the truck was full of asphalt! That oversight almost killed them. An investigation later determined that with that weight, at that altitude, they should not have been able to get airborne. Obviously, God was not finished with them.

Because of shortage of qualified pilots, some were called back to flying duties after years of being out of the cockpit. As a navigator, my brother was once assigned to a crew with two of these veteran pilots.

As they were preparing for the flight, the following conversation took place:

> Pilot #1: I would just as soon be the co-pilot today because my eyes aren't that good anymore and I don't want to do the landings.
> Pilot #2: That works for me. My hearing is shot so I wouldn't be any good on the radios.

Somehow, they survived that day.

On the other hand, an older lieutenant colonel was their aircraft commander for some months. Unlike many of the young pilots, he was very cautious because he didn't feel he had anything to prove. One day, my brother's aircraft was part of a large operation. The group was headed toward a difficult runway, down in a valley, surrounded by steep hills loaded with Viet Cong. The younger guys took it as a mark of pride to make a perfect approach and landing the first time because there was a crowd on the ground critiquing their performance. But this A/C was not suffering from any false pride. He went around four times before he was totally satisfied with his approach. He couldn't care less about what any of the other pilots thought of him. My brother, for one, was grateful for his caution.

My brother went on to finish his career in the Air Force, retiring as a major. I am very proud of him and his service for our country.

THE POEM

By Kathy Carroll Earnshaw
El Camino Real Chapter, NSDAR/now Los Gatos Chapter, NSDAR
Los Gatos, California

I had just learned that I was pregnant when the news arrived that my brother, Timmy, was missing in action. I remember thinking, "Don't worry, he will be okay." We played "Cowboys and Indians" when we were kids. and he always won.

My brother, Timothy Michael Carroll, was born August 1, 1944, and raised in San José, a ninth generation Californian. He was the second child and only son of William and Geraldine (Perry) Carroll. Until leaving for Vietnam, he worked for his dad, a San José cattle rancher. He was a good looking young man, tall with dark hair and blue eyes. Family members and friends called him "Tim" or "Timmy."

Private Timothy M. Carroll
United States Army

Timmy grew up in the Evergreen and Almaden areas of San José, attending Evergreen Elementary School and Pioneer High School. I am two years older than him. We also had three younger sisters, Karen, Patricia, and Edith.

Timmy was a lefty, and a natural athlete. He loved Elvis Presley music, all sports, and fast cars. When he wasn't driving one of the old pickup trucks on the ranch, he drove a 1962 red Corvette. Girls were always calling him, but he was a shy young man, and often quiet.

However, his friends were so numerous that it took six San José motorcycle officers to escort the funeral entourage from the funeral home to Oak Hill Cemetery. It usually takes just two officers. According to officials, it was the largest funeral San José had ever seen. I remember sitting in the hearse and looking down Monterey Highway. As far as I could see, there were cars with their headlights on. Lots of people along the side of the road were holding flags. It was almost like being in a parade. It was Timmy's parade.

Timmy was reported missing in action on March 9, 1969, only a few months before his 25th birthday. For two days we prayed that he would be found alive. He was six feet two inches tall, with a size thirteen shoe. He was so strong, we just knew he would be okay. But on the third day, the Army informed us that he had been killed.

His bunker had taken a direct hit from the shellings coming into Vietnam from Cambodia. He had served as Private First Class in the 5th Battalion, 16th Artillery, 4th Infantry Division of the United States Army. He was awarded the Bronze Star, the Army Commendation Medal, the Purple Heart, and the Good Conduct Medal. He had been in Vietnam nine months and was due to come home in three months.

Timmy did not want to go to Vietnam, but he was drafted, so he went and he served. Once he was there, he often wrote home about the Vietnamese children and what was happening. He said the Vietnamese needed the Americans and that what we were doing was right. While there, he looked out for a little boy who was about nine years old and talked of bringing the boy home with him. Of course, this would have been impossible, but Timmy was used to doing the impossible. Did he die in vain? This is a question that his family and friends will always ask.

In April 1987, my sister, Karen Ellner, and I established the Timothy Michael Carroll Fund. Both of us were members of the El Camino Real Chapter of the Daughters of the American Revolution, as was Timmy's mother, Geraldine Carroll Wilson, and his aunt, Dorothy Floren. This fund was started to ensure that the chapter would always have funds available to finance its work with disabled veterans. Timmy's name is on the Vietnam Veterans Memorial Wall in Washington, D.C., as well as on the California Vietnam Veterans Memorial in Sacramento. His name and face will always be a part of our memories. Shortly after he was killed, our Mom wrote this short poem she titled simply, "Tim":

There was a lump in my throat and a tear in my eye
He put his arms around me and held me to him
He was my only son and his name was Tim
He was so tall and so handsome in his army uniform
He was trying to be brave, but I knew his heart was torn
No, he didn't want to go, to fight in this war and I wondered if I'd
    ever see my son Tim anymore
So he went to Viet Nam, and so many letters he did write
And they all said, "Don't worry Mom, everything is alright"
I missed him so much and I worried so
He made some good friends there, another Tim also Bobbie and Joe
Then the rockets started falling and to their bunkers they did run
When it was all over, they would never see another sun
So the last letter I got said again "Hey Mom please don't worry"
I'll be home before long, and I'm sure in a hurry
But the doorbell rang, and a Captain stood there that day
He didn't have to talk, I knew what he would say
Yes, my young son had given his life,
For a country so torn and so full of strife
It took twelve days to get him back home
Again by himself and so all alone
There was our American flag, it was draped on his coffin
My God, I couldn't believe it, I'd worried so often
They opened the coffin and I looked down at him
He was so handsome and with ribbons on his chest
He'd gone where he didn't want to go and he did his best.
I wanted to hold him and kiss him once more.
But I couldn't because of something called the "Viet Nam" war.
There was Scott & Peter, Dickie, Elroy and then Jim,
They carried the body of their good friend Tim.
So now at the grave yard, I spend the hours
Sitting and thinking, arranging the flowers
May you rest in peace now and worry no more
Your life came to an end because of a war.

THE SEQUOIA HIGH SCHOOL MEMORIAL

By Dee Eva
La Puerta de Oro-San Francisco Chapter, NSDAR
San Francisco, California

The Sequoia Veterans Memorial monument project started in October 2001, right after the September 11 attacks on New York's World Trade Center and the Pentagon. My husband and I were talking about a memorial to those who died in the attack, and he suggested a memorial at Sequoia High School in Redwood City, California, honoring all students who died while serving in the military. We both attended Sequoia High School and graduated in 1961.

The Sequoia High School Veterans Memorial
Sequoia High School, Redwood City, Califormia

We had three Sequoia High School friends who died during the Vietnam War. Their names were not on the Vietnam Memorial in Washington, D.C., because they did not die in combat. Our classmate, Ted Sweeting, had been a friend since seventh grade. He was a fighter pilot. He was shot down over Vietnam, rescued the next day, and sent to Amsterdam to recover from his injuries. While recovering, he and his co-pilot flew to another country for a visit. On their way back, just outside of Amsterdam, their plane crashed. They were both killed. Our good friend, Kenny Quinn, was part of a helicopter flight crew in Vietnam. He served three tours of duty and was about to be discharged when he was killed in an automobile accident. Our classmate, Fred Zentil, was in the Air Force in Texas. He was assigned to clean out the inside of a plane's wings when the plane exploded, and he was killed.

As I started researching those who attended Sequoia High School and died while in military service, I learned that the Sequoia High School Alumni Association had a list of military alumni going back to WWI. The majority of them died in active duty during WWII.

I asked if the school district and school personnel would be interested in having a monument on the campus honoring Sequoia High School students. I was told they would very much like that kind of memorial and was told to contact the head of the grounds-keeping crew to choose a site. The crew had a site in a prominent location near the flagpole that was perfect for the memorial. At that time, they were trying to find a use for the site. Perfect timing!

I approached a local monument company for the monument's design and construction. The final design included the insignias of the different branches of the military, all centered around the Sequoia High School insignia. The names of 106 Sequoia High School alumni who died while in military service were to be engraved below the insignia cluster.

While the monument was being fabricated, I worked with the alumni association, gathering more names for the monument. I appealed to the alumni for monetary donations. I attended meetings of local community service and volunteer groups, asking for support and donations. It took several years to fund the project. We sold engraved bricks that were installed in a patio around the monument, bronze plaques attached to boulders next to trees planted around the grounds of the monument, and engraved concrete benches that were placed around the patio and pathway to the monument. The school district planted grass around the memorial, several cherry and redwood trees, and numerous red and white roses. The district also installed a pathway and lighting for the monument and continues to maintain the grounds.

The committee to plan the dedication ceremony consisted of Sequoia High School alumni: my husband and I, Julie Salas (president of the Peninsula Hills Women's Club), Dr. Olivia Martinez (a member of the Sequoia Union High School District Board of Trustees), Dr. Jeffrey Filippi (one of the founders of the Sequoia High School Alumni Association), Carolyn Abbott Livengood (a reporter for the *San Mateo County Times*), Robert Page (quartermaster, Veterans of Foreign Wars), James Lindsay Wilson (VFW Post 2310), and City Council Member Diane Howard.

We publicized the ceremony in press releases, in *Smoke Signals*, (the alumni association newsletter), and sent invitations to everyone who donated to the project. Nearly 800 people attended. The ceremony included a military band, a flag-folding ceremony, presentation of various proclamations, and military honors. Major Kim Sweeting McArthur, United States Air Force, daughter of our classmate, Ted Sweeting, attended the ceremony. It was the first such ceremony honoring her father, and she felt she needed to be there. She was just a small child when her father died, and her younger sister was born a few months after his death. Kim read the wording for the flag folding portion of the ceremony.

While planning the ceremony, I was contacted by a New Jersey attorney who said he had read a compilation of letters from American soldiers stationed in Vietnam. He was so touched by one of the letters, he carried a copy of it in his wallet. The letter was written by David Callis (Sequoia High School, 1963), a casualty of the Vietnam War. Coincidentally, David's sister and I grew up together. I put the attorney and the sister in touch, and she gave him the original of the letter he had carried for many years. I invited him to attend the dedication ceremony, to speak about finding the letter and how it had touched him. He and his wife flew out for the ceremony. He gave a moving speech about the impact David's words had on him. Those in attendance were mesmerized by what he said.

Since the completion of the memorial project, we have had two more names engraved on the monument: one a casualty in Afghanistan, and one a soldier who was home from Afghanistan and died in an accident. As we do more research, we have at least three or four more names to be engraved from World War II. We are still selling bricks, trees, and benches. The proceeds from those sales go to "Cherokee Grants," funds given to teachers for classroom supplies, field trips, in-service training and for student needs.

LETTER FROM DAVID CALLIS

This is the letter from David Callis to his parents, referred to in the previous story. The letter is an excerpt from a compilation of letters written by military personnel while serving in Vietnam. The compilation is currently out of print.

Marine Pfc. David Callis wrote this letter to his parents in Redwood City, California, expressing his belief in the necessity for the continuation of the struggle in Vietnam, in spite of its horrors. David Callis was killed in action during March, 1966.

Dear everyone in my world:

Tonight is the eve of combat. Tomorrow morning I embark on my first real journey into the unknown, from my own world of nineteen years into the cruel and savage arena of hatred and bloodshed that is called war. We have replaced the blanks with bullets, the lifeless, harmless dummies with metallic missles capable of quick death and destruction. Everything we now have goes off with a big boom. And with each boom people will die.

The jungle, heat, mud, snakes, leeches, insects, and Viet Cong become my adversaries, each one greedily eager to tear at me and snuff out my life. Only God's will and my training as a Marine give me the chance to survive. But I feel I will live to fight another day and fight to live another day. I will survive. I will come home.

Most of us, if not all of us know that the whole world is watching this country that none of us knew before. We all know it is war, and that the stakes are high, maybe higher than we can understand. We also know that there are no winners, only losers. Some will die that others may live. The losers will find rest in some Vietnam jungle grave. The winners will come home again one day, a little older, a little haggard and battle weary, but a lot wiser. Theirs will not be the victory of battle, but the triumph of humility and an appreciation of life itself, of all we hold to be good and true and noble.

If I should be a loser, my memory will live on in you and I will be part of a bigger memory in those who love what is right. If I lose, please don't mourn, but be proud that in my small way I won something for you and all those who love freedom.

I am not afraid, only somewhat apprehensive. Come to think of it, I'd rather die from a Viet Cong bullet than under the wheels of a speeding car.

Please join me in a prayer for a better tomorrow when the horrors of war and the infamy of men will belong to a forgotten people in a forgotten past.

God bless all of you at home. You're fighting the war in your hearts, with the anguish of watching and waiting, hoping only that your prayers for us will be answered.

Now I ask our Father to grant my prayer mercifully for another place and another time without war.

I love you all very much.

Your son and brother,
David

FLYING FOR CONTINENTAL AIRLINES

By Alice Ganley
Anne Loucks Chapter, NSDAR
Martinez, California

I was an air hostess or stewardess/flight attendant for Continental Airlines during the Vietnam War. Continental Airlines and Flying Tiger Airlines were the two major components of the Military Airlift Command, flying troops in and out of Vietnam.

Just before one of my flights, Braniff Airlines entered into a contract for a few flights. Unfortunately, for their first flight they chose to use one of their pumpkin orange airplanes. American military pilots wore pumpkin orange jumpsuits. The North Vietnamese and the Chinese paid a bounty for anything pumpkin orange that was captured. Also, unfortunately, Braniff had a pilot who landed that pumpkin orange airplane as if he were landing at San Francisco Airport - low and slow. The usual manner for landing our planes in Vietnam was to come in at a high altitude and high speed.

Alice Ganley
Air Hostess, Continental Airlines

The pilot then made a very steep dive for the end of the runway and immediately stood on the brakes, throwing the engines into reverse thrust, and throwing up the wing flaps to get stopped on a relatively short runway. After the Braniff flight left, every one of our planes going in or out of Vietnam was shot at with increased frequency.

Our planes leaving Vietnam often left with holes in the fuselage and vertical stabilizers. When we were on Guam for refueling, the captain took me to the rear of the plane and pointed out a large hole just inches away from the hydraulic lines in the vertical stabilizer. We were very blessed to still have control of the airplane. The captain asked, "Why do you think I sit on the metal flight log?" I didn't stop to think until later that he was kidding me. That thin metal flight log would have been no protection at all.

Another flight left Vietnam just days after a member of the Vietnamese cabin cleaning crew was caught planting a bomb under the captain's seat. He was taken just far enough from the plane that no bullets would ricochet and damage the plane, and he was shot - swift justice. After that, no Vietnamese were allowed near the planes.

Air hostesses were not allowed off the airplanes while we were in Vietnam. We were not even allowed near the doors and windows. We had to have enough fuel on board the plane to get to Vietnam and get back to a safe location for refueling, because in Vietnam no fuel trucks were allowed near the airplanes.

It took sixteen hours to fly from the United States to Vietnam. The flights to Vietnam often had a party atmosphere. The military passengers were on a four-engine passenger jet with air hostesses on board. We made extensions for the headsets so that they could hear the music and there was dancing in the aisles. Some of the more senior air hostesses made dozens of cookies for each trip they flew. We played cards. Mostly we talked. Before landing, there was always the moment when you looked at those young men and women and wondered how many were going to be coming home, or how many would be missing arms, legs, or have other grievous injuries.

On the way home, the flights were extremely quiet. My flights from Vietnam were at a time when the people being rotated out were kept in tents the night before their flight home. There were even occasions when some confused, disillusioned troops would throw grenades into those sleeping quarters. The troops on the planes out of Vietnam were so afraid that something would happen so close to getting home safely that they didn't move out of their seats. When we touched ground at Travis Air Force Base, there was a cheer that shook the airplane. As the troops got to the bottom of the steps, they bent down on hands and knees and kissed the tarmac.

FROM THE CORNFIELDS OF ILLINOIS

By Barbara Irwin Gildea
Presidio Chapter, NSDAR
San Francisco, California

My dad was a Vietnam veteran. His name was Jesse A. Irwin and he was a colonel in the United States Air Force.

Colonel Jesse A. Irwin
United States Air Force

In 1963, I was in the fifth grade. My world was a small town outside Scott Air Force Base in Illinois. I attended Catholic school in that town. Fourth of July fireworks and trips to the commissary are my on-base memories.

My father, with few exceptions, arrived home from his overseas trips late at night. We always awoke to him fixing breakfast and the living room full of unusual gifts from different parts of the world. I remember my teacher, who was also a family friend, stopping the class one morning and announcing, "Barbara Irwin, you should be very grateful that your father came home last night." I did not know where my father had been, but it was my first introduction to the fact that my dad had a dangerous job.

In the summer of 1964, we moved to Hickam Air Force Base in Hawaii. It was the first time in my twelve years that we moved with my father to his new assignment instead of staying behind in Mascoutah, Illinois, where my dad had returned between his temporary duty assignments.

As vice commander, then commander, of MAC (Military Airlift

Command) 61st Support Wing from 1964-1968, he was responsible for flying troops and equipment from Hickam Air Force Base to Southeast Asia. For my siblings and me, the world was our Catholic schools. Star of the Sea High School, on the Diamond Head side of the island, was an all-girls school that required saddle oxfords and blue plaid skirts. It was very removed from the war. Our free time was spent at Fort DeRussy at Waikiki. When I was a little older, we would drive to Makapu'u and body surf all day.

My dad had a red phone at his bedside and a very large walkie-talkie with him at all times. He never talked much about his job, and when he spoke of danger, he was able to put a humorous spin on it. He once told us how his plane was shelled by mortar fire while taxiing down the runway leaving Da Nang. The crew piled out and took shelter in a one-man guard post. He made it sound like one of those elephant jokes. That was my dad. He was larger than life - very handsome and very funny. The most serious conversation I had with him about the war was when he told me that officers in Da Nang did not want to wear their insignia to the mess tent before meals because snipers always picked off the officers first.

In 1966, during Easter vacation, my father took my sisters and me on the most wonderful two-week trip to Japan. I assumed that he was on business, yet it felt as though we had him all to ourselves. We flew to Japan, "space available," on United Airlines and flew home, after a stop in the Philippines, on a transport plane packed with Army soldiers. Some were on their way to a rest and recuperation leave in Hawaii, while others were returning home from the war. Dad insisted that we walk from the rear of the plane where we were seated all the way to the cockpit so that we could meet the pilot and crew. I will never forget that moment. There were many eyes focused on the colonel's three teen-aged daughters.

I did not learn until decades later, after my father had passed away, that he was made an honorary member of the U.S. Army 25th Infantry Division, Tropic Lightning. According to a conversation I had with United States Army General Fred C. Weyand, my dad was awarded this honor for his role in Operation Blue Light, one of the largest military troop and equipment transport operations of that time. Of all my dad's accomplishments, he confided in me that he was most proud of his role in Operation Blue Light, even though he never talked about the specifics.

High Award For 349th Commander

Colonel Jesse A. Irwin, 349th Military Airlift Wing commander at Hamilton Air Force Base, has been awarded the Legion of Merit for exceptionally meritorious conduct in the performance of outstanding service to the United States.

The nation's seventh highest award was presented to Colonel Irwin for his service with the 61st Military Airlift Wing from July, 1964, through June this year.

Colonel Irwin, a veteran of 28 years of service and a native of Auburn, Ill., became commander of the 349th "Golden Gate" Wing in July, 1968.

Prior to this, he was vice commander and then commander of the 61st Military Airlift Wing at Hickam Air Force Base, Hawaii.

He and his wife Mary have five children. The Irwins reside at 798 Rowland Drive, Novato.

COL. JESSE A. IRWIN
Awarded Legion Of Merit

Article provided by Barbara Gildea. Date and source of publication unknown.

From 1968 to 1970, my father was commander of the 349th Air Mobility Wing at Hamilton Air Force Base, Marin County, California. The huge C-141 and other transport aircraft were too big for Hamilton's runways, so my father flew out of Travis Air Force Base. Once again, he was gone all the time.

By the time Dad retired in 1970, he was sick of the war. He never said that. He didn't have to. I knew that flying home from Vietnam with all those soldiers in body bags broke his heart. After he retired, he never flew again. He told me he just got tired of it. This from someone who, when I was a small child, used to borrow a small, four-seater plane from a family friend and take off from the cornfields of Illinois to visit Grandma and Grandpa.

A VIEW OF THE WAR FROM CARMEL

By Betsy Haslett
Captain Henry Sweetser Chapter, NSDAR
Santa Maria, California

My family lived in Carmel on the Monterey Peninsula, with Fort Ord several miles away. In nearby Monterey, there was a large popular roller skating rink where, thanks to the Vietnam War, my sister met her future husband. Recently, they celebrated their forty-ninth wedding anniversary. My sister is ten years older than I am. In high school, my sister and my third-grade teacher were enrolled in the same German language class.

From a third-grader perspective in 1965, my teacher talked often enough about the war to my class. She was engaged to a soldier. At a class reunion many years later, several of us were talking about our third-grade teacher, Miss Byrnes, as she was a favorite teacher for many of us. A classmate reminded me of how she had us write letters to soldiers.

There was one night I recall anticipating. Visitors were to be allowed into Fort Ord to listen to combat practice. The observation area was on the other side of a sand dune or hill, so all I remember is noise and seeing the red glare of gunfire.

After my newly married sister moved to Germany (due to her husband's transfer order), I have fewer memories of the war for about two years. My school district decided to have fifth and sixth-graders go to junior high school, and my class of fifth graders was the first to move up. My sixth-grade art teacher offered to teach guitar to interested students, and I was one who was interested. He spoke often of his views of the Vietnam War. He opposed the war.

Then a day came when those who opposed the Vietnam War were supposed to wear a black armband. On that day, I put black bands around both my elbows and both my knees. That afternoon I went outside to help my mother at the car. My mother had a certain tone of voice when she spoke very quietly, and I knew I had to obey. She took one look at me and said, "You have no idea what that means." I do not recall when or where I removed those four black bands. It must have been soon afterward, and I never wore them again.

My sister, her husband, and their new son returned after two years in Germany. When her husband's orders for Vietnam eventually came through, she and he decided that she and their son, then age two, would go to live in a small town in Idaho, near his eldest brother's cattle ranch. I visited her in Idaho a few times.

A few years after my brother-in-law's return from Vietnam, he was transferred to South Carolina. When I was fourteen, my mother and I went to visit them. According to a few conversations I overheard about his nightmares, and some behaviors I personally witnessed, my brother-in-law was probably experiencing whatis now referred to as post traumatic stress disorder. My sister was very upset and told our mother that she was afraid of a divorce (our parents were divorced nearly ten years at this time).

Soldiers were a common sight all around the Monterey Peninsula. In high school, my girlfriends and I were a quiet, studious bunch. We did not encourage passes from soldiers stationed at Fort Ord. It was usually easy to spot who the soldiers were because of their hair-cuts. There was a time when many of the enlisted men even tried to wear wigs when they were off base for free time. The Monterey area was also known for being a hippie migration/hitchhiking route south to the Big Sur coast. So, yes, hair and clothing styles were telling.

In high school, I was caught up in my studies and usually tuned out the Vietnam War. Then the war was over. Recently, while looking at historical records, I realized that the war ended in 1975, about three weeks prior to my high school graduation.

Because of my time serving in the Daughters of the American Revolution with a Service for Veterans Committee, I more deeply appreciate our veterans. I rode on a float my chapter had in a local Veterans Day Parade the year the theme was "Welcome Home, Vietnam Vets."

Basic Training at Fort Ord, California
Photo from the *Telegram-Tribune*, November 9, 1966
San Luis Obispo, California

MAJOR MORRISON ARTHUR COTNER

By Genevieve Marie Hassan
El Redondo Chapter, NSDAR
Redondo Beach, California

My husband, Morrison Arthur Cotner, was a major in the United States Air Force. He served in the Vietnam War from August 1966 to April 27, 1967, the day he was killed by the Viet Cong. At the time of his death, he was forty-one years old. He was a forward air controller, and the liaison officer for the United States Air Force to a Division of the South Korean Army that was helping the United States fight the Chinese Communists in Vietnam.

When he died, Morrison was flying his Piper Cub over Viet Cong enemy territory about fifty feet above the ground. The Viet Cong had been ambushing the South Koreans when they were on patrol. Morrison and the Air Force photographer with him spotted the Viet Cong cave where the enemy was hiding. The Viet Cong shot down Morrison's small plane with machine gun fire. The plane went down in the South China Sea.

Morrison was posthumously awarded the Silver Star. Prior to his Vietnam service, he had received the

Major Morrison Arthur Cotner
United States Air Force

Bronze Star and two Air Medals. The South Korean government also awarded him its Medal of Valor for his services to the nation.

Almost every day before his death, I received a tape from Morrison, telling me about the progress of the war and inquiring about how we were doing at home. I lived in constant terror that something bad would happen to him at any time. He lived in a tent, and most of the time I could hear shells from the enemy flying overhead on the tapes he sent. I still have boxes of his tapes, but have never listened to them again. It would be too painful. We met each other in Hawaii for his rest and recreation just two weeks before he died.

Before he went to Vietnam, Morrison received his training to be a forward air controller at Eglin Air Force Base, Fort Walton Beach, Florida. Our four children and I went with him to Florida for his three months of training. Our three older children, who were then ten, eight, and five years old, remember their beloved and fun-loving father from that summer in Florida and the years before. Our youngest child was only two years old. She does not remember her father at all.

Morrison had been a fighter pilot all of his previous career in the United States Air Force. He flew jets in the Korean War from May 1952 until June 1953. Prior to joining the Air Force in 1951, he was in the Reserve Officers' Training Corps at the University of Arkansas, where he received his B.A. degree. He was a lieutenant colonel in the Reserves and was planning to retire from military service when he returned from Vietnam. The three years before he was sent to Vietnam, he was stationed at the El Segundo Space Station and attached to what was then North American (now Boeing) as an engineer and test pilot. North American had offered him civilian employment as soon as he returned from Vietnam.

Before the El Segundo facility, we lived in Stillwater, Oklahoma, while Morrison attended Oklahoma State University. That is where he obtained his aeronautical engineering degree. At that time, he kept himself on flying status by going up to Tinker Air Force Base in Oklahoma City a couple of days each month. Previous to Stillwater, we lived for four and a half years at Cannon Air Force Base in Clovis, New Mexico. This location is where squadrons of fighter pilots were stationed. Morrison's prior Air Force training took place at Ardmore Air Force Base, Oklahoma;

Del Rio Air Force Base, Texas; and Nellis Air Force Base in Las Vegas, Nevada.

To round out the story of his military career, Morrison was also in the Navy in World War II as a very young sailor. He joined when he was only sixteen years old. He served on a destroyer tender from 1942 to 1945 in the South Pacific.

Morrison served his country long and well. He should not have been sent to fight in the Vietnam War. This was a war that I feel was wrong for the United States to become involved with in the first place.

LOOKING BACK

By Norma Andersen Hayden
Sierra Amador Chapter, NSDAR
Jackson, California

In March of 1965, nearing the end of my junior year in high school, the stress in my life consisted of junior prom, summer plans, and senior year classes. At home, I never missed the evening news with Walter Cronkite. Over the previous months, he talked of an increase of United States troops and military advisors in Vietnam. My future husband, Hugh Hayden, whom I would meet in another three years, was about to enter a dangerous period in his life.

Hugh Hayden, July 1965
An Ton, Chu Lai, Vietnam

In March of 1965, the life of my future husband was abruptly changed. He had been stationed at the Marine base in Kaneohe, Hawaii, enjoying military life on an island paradise, when his battalion was given a new assignment. He soon found himself on a troop transport heading to Vietnam as part of the first Marine ground troops going ashore at China Beach.

Over the summer and into the fall of 1965, fatherly Walter Cronkite calmly reported soldier losses in Vietnam. I did not share the concerns and fears of others since I had no brothers, no male cousins, and no uncles young enough to be called to serve in the war.

In July of 1965, Hugh was in Chu Lai, Vietnam. In August, he fought alongside his Marine brothers in Operation Starlight, the first major offensive by United States ground forces.

By December of 1965, the evening news was covering the Vietnam conflict with film and still photos. I recall Walter Cronkite's somber reports. At this time I was focused on high school graduation and readying for college. The boys in my graduating class were beginning to pay close attention to the war as they each in turn attained the age of eighteen and were required to register for selective service. There was talk about how to make sure they went to college to avoid the draft. Simon and Garfunkel produced a song titled, "7 O'clock News/Silent Night," that made a profound statement. The song was so poignant, so truthful. Some took the song as a protest against the war, and it might have been, but I did not. For me, it spoke honestly of how we can simultaneously be joyous and terribly sad.

In December of 1965, my future husband, Hugh, was in Chu Lai. A group photo was taken of his platoon at that time. He celebrated his twenty-first birthday under mortar attack from the Viet Cong while defending the platoon's base of operation. In February of 1966, immediately after returning from a patrol, his commanding officer told him his tour was up, and there was a chopper taking off in five minutes - if he hurried he could catch it. He arrived in Da Nang with only the clothes on his back. After a shower to wash off the jungle sweat, he was issued some fatigues and flown to Okinawa. All of his possessions had been lost in an attack. He was left with nothing of his own.

After a ten-day stay to treat an illness he was placed on a commercial airliner headed to the United States. Talk about culture shock! When he flew home from El Toro, California, he was told for his own safety not to wear his uniform in the airport. How difficult it was for him to hear that his service, his war injury, the deaths of his Marine brothers, were not only not honored, they were reviled.

In the fall of 1967, I attended the local junior college. The draft was in the future, and students were worried. There were discussions about how to keep their student deferments by possibly going to Canada, or declaring themselves as "conscientious objectors." Those less able to afford school, or unable to keep up their grade averages, were going to be subject to the draft. They were scared.

By 1969, demonstrations against returning veterans became common. There were speeches against the war at my college and flag burning events in nearby cities. I was engaged to my Marine by that time, and I was proud of his service. He was quiet about his time on the front lines and cautioned me against saying he was a Vietnam veteran. He would not reveal that he was a Purple Heart veteran.

Protests against the war frightened me. The anger at the servicemen was so misplaced, but to argue with a dissenter was nonproductive. Then I learned of high school classmates who gave their lives in Vietnam. It was hard to believe they were gone at such a young age. The final, horrific sight was watching the airlift from a rooftop in Saigon when the city was being overrun.

To this day, I am very proud of my Marine Vietnam veteran husband. A few years ago, he attended a reunion of the 2nd Battalion, 4th Marines, and was able to visit with some of those with whom he served in Vietnam. He gave them all quite a shock. They had heard he was killed during a firefight. After exchanging recollections with several of the guys, he was able to piece together the whole story. As the company radio operator, his radio became inoperable, and he was injured in the first wave of fighting. Unbeknownst to his soldier brothers, a replacement radio operator went up in the observation tower and was killed by a mortar attack. They assumed it was my husband when it was reported that the company radio operator had been killed.

Echo Company, 2nd Battalion, 4th Marines
Chu Lai, December 1965

MY COUSIN DONALD

By Thelma Hayes
La Cuesta Chapter, NSDAR
San Luis Obispo, California

During the Vietnam War, I was a military wife and the mother of two children stationed at several overseas locations. Nashville, Tennessee, was my hometown. My extended family on my mother's side with the surname, Douglas, included my grandparents, an aunt, five uncles and twenty cousins. I had two uncles who served our country during WWII (one in the Army, one in the Navy), and one uncle served during the Korean War in the Army. Only one of my cousins, Donald Douglas, served during the Vietnam War. He was in the Marine Corps on the front lines.

Donald Douglas and sentry dog, Nick. Da Nang, Vietnam, 1968

In the fall of 1964 my husband, Gary Hegwood, was assigned to the 498th Tactical Missile Group at Kadena Air Force Base on Okinawa. His work assignment was missle maintenance. We lived in a local residential area known as Machinato. We had an Okinawan maid named Miyoko, who became an important part of our family. She loved our sons, showering them with affection and constant attention. Because I had excellent household help, I decided to work outside the home. I obtained a civilian position with the Army that required a top secret clearance. The United States Army ran a telecommunications center located on a small Marine base near my home. In that position, I operated cryptographic equipment and processed communications.

Through family correspondence, I was aware that my cousin Donald served on the front lines in Vietnam. I was very concerned for his safety. Late in the year 1965, I received news that the ship taking him to the United States would be stopping in Okinawa for a couple of days. I was very happy to learn that he was safe, healthy and heading back to our hometown. I was also overjoyed that he would be able to visit with me en route.

The Hegwood Family in Machinato, Okinawa, 1966.
Left to right: Gary, Tim, Thelma and Jeff.

The day finally arrived, and we were able to spend time together halfway around the world. Donald fell in love with my two sons, and I thought, "He will make a great dad when he has children of his own."

As a young mother, my culinary attempts left much to be desired. My failures included cooking a whole turkey for the first time, and leaving the giblets in the plastic bag inside the bird. On this special occasion, I decided to serve familiar Southern dishes to Donald and my little family: meat loaf, green beans, corn, mashed potatoes and gravy, cornbread, and sweet tea. Apparently, my skills were improving since the meal was enjoyed by all.

At the time of Donald's visit, my boys, Tim and Jeff, were four years old and eighteen months. As Douglas and I talked on and on about our families and our memories, Tim decided to wander outside to ride his much loved bike. Pretty soon the rattle of his bike going down the unpaved, gravel road grew quite loud and sharp. Donald reacted instantly as if there was great danger connected with the noise coming from outside. When he calmed down, Donald explained that the sound was exactly the same as rapid machine gunfire. He had reacted instinctively, just as he would have on the front lines. His reaction touched me deeply. Today, I would give him a big hug and hold him tightly. However, at that time, our families weren't accustomed to showing open affection. Neither were we aware of the term, PTSD (post traumatic stress disorder), that affects many servicemen and women.

Thankfully, Donald returned to Tennessee, his wonderful parents and six siblings to lead a peaceful and productive life. Today, he's a California transplant like me. He and his wife live in San Marcos. My home is in San Luis Obispo. My older son, Tim, lives with his large family in Dallas, Texas. His younger brother, Jeff, resides with his small family in San Diego, within twenty miles of my cousin Donald's home.

EVERY GENERATION HAS ITS WAR

By Susan Holder
Gold Trail Chapter, NSDAR
Roseville, California

I believe every generation has its war. Vietnam is mine.

My earliest memory was from the sixth grade in Los Angeles where we shared "current events." I chose a small newspaper clipping about Vietnam and how the French were there as advisors and now the United States was escalating its involvement. It was a very small article. Little did I know how large and frightening this little-known country would turn out to be in our nation's history.

Fast forward to high school in Santa Cruz, California, 1967-1970. I was becoming increasingly aware of this unpopular conflict. How could I not be aware? Santa Cruz was a miniature Berkeley, and my days of innocence were fading as the war loomed over everyone of that generation. I faithfully watched the nightly news about Vietnam, and, as the anchor announced the broadcast date, I reflected on my ordinary day. Then my thoughts turned to those young boys fighting in a foreign land.

There were two preeminent Vietnam era events in the late 1960's that had an impact on me: the lottery draft by birth date and the Bob Hope Christmas Specials. When the draft lottery dates were announced, we eagerly read the newspaper with our male friends to locate where their birthdays ranked. I had friends who ranked in the top ten, a definite ticket to Vietnam. Others were located towards the end of the lottery, and they would let out big sighs of relief. Some enlisted in the Coast Guard or Navy because they didn't want to be involved in the ground fighting. Still others were so-called "draft dodgers." It wasn't because they were not patriotic, but because the stories of drug abuse in Vietnam were scarier than the actual fighting. A few guys took the legal way to fight the draft; one friend was even victorious in federal court (due to a technicality) under the counsel of attorney Gary Patton, who would later become the mayor of Santa Cruz.

But year after year, it was the Bob Hope Christmas Specials that got to me the most. I would sit there and cry as the camera panned on those soldiers. They were just boys. Many of them couldn't even vote. The voting age was twenty-one then, not eighteen as it is today. They all looked so young, not old enough to be fighting that war. How many would never return home again? It left a huge pit in my stomach.

The Vietnam conflict continued as the protests raged on. Eventually in the spring of 1975, I was a young wife and mother. The United States was pulling out of Vietnam as Saigon fell to the North Vietnamese. The South Vietnamese citizens were fleeing by any means possible, clinging onto helicopters from rooftops, desperate to leave the country. The images were incredible. This conflict was over, but it left lingering questions for years.

It is now 2015 and Lani, from Vietnam, has been beautifully taking care of my nails in a spa salon for the past fifteen years. Her father was a policeman in Vietnam and was killed by the Cambodians the day she was born. This was long before the United States involvement. She was raised by her mother, who labored in the oil fields. Lani married a soldier while he was serving in Vietnam and in 1975, she was able to move to the United States with him and their son. Lani is the sweetest and dearest person, and I am honored to call her my friend.

Yes, Vietnam is my war. It left an indelible mark on those who served, on the families whose loved ones never returned, on those who left Vietnam and started a new life in the United States, and on all of us who have lived through those life-changing times.

"I HOPE I HELPED"

By Sue-Ellen Hollahan
San Fernando Valley Chapter, NSDAR
San Fernando, California

I was raised in a military family. My father was a graduate of West Point and a career Air Force officer. My brother was also in the service. I felt it was my duty to honor and respect those who were serving our country. Many of my high school friends were sent to Vietnam while I was in college.

After school in 1970, I began my career as a National Airlines flight attendant. At that time there were still many opinions about the Vietnam War, and I will never forget the first trip that I worked going into San Francisco. Seeing the protesters and anti-war slogans everywhere made me feel uncomfortable and unsure of what I could do.

While walking through San Francisco International Airport, we encountered groups protesting the war. These groups berated all of the young men and women in uniform who were on their way overseas. They screamed horrible names at military personnel and treated them like they were the enemy! From that point on, every chance I had, I went out of my way to be respectful

Sue-Ellen Hollahan
National Airlines
Flight Attendant

and do whatever I could to be accommodating to the military personnel that I had on my flights. Whether it was to offer them extra food and drink (complementary, of course) or a pillow or blanket, my small tokens of appreciation were always accepted with a "Thank you, ma'am".

I hope in a small way, I helped them realize that not all Americans blamed them for the events that they had to take part in, and that their service was appreciated.

LIFE AS A MILITARY WIFE WASN'T EASY

By Barbara Jean Holland
Tomo-Kahni Chapter, NSDAR
Tehachapi, California

I am a Vietnam era civilian who was touched not only by how the war began, but by my husband's service in the United States Army. I was by his side.

My high school class of 1963 was the last group of what I call "the innocents." My senior year represented high school memories, college ahead, and the ending of my mother's battle with cancer. In high school, I became excited about politics. First, there was the Nixon-Kennedy presidential campaign, then Kennedy's victory. Studying the Constitution was exciting. Then we experienced the Cuban missile crisis. Rumors began about a war starting up in Southeast Asia. Then President Kennedy was assassinated, and the world seemed to be spinning uncontrollably. President Johnson talked about sending more troops to Vietnam. The war pushed forward, yet stumbled. Later on, we learned that our military hands had been tied by politics.

I was beginning to lose my naiveté. Keeping our country safe was utmost in my mind. Sad news came each time a local soldier was killed. Never did I think I would be affected by a war on the other side of the world, but I was.

In 1965, I met a young man in church named Jack Holland. In 1967, we were married in the church where we met. Jack had studied at the University of California, Berkeley. He had to leave school and returned home because his father had died. Jack took a job as a postman to support his mother and sister. August 1967, Jack received word that he had been accepted back to Berkeley. We were thrilled. That was on a Friday night. We celebrated. Saturday afternoon, Jack's mother called to say he should come over right away. He received the letter from President Johnson that he had been drafted into the United States Army and was to leave for boot camp at Fort Ord. We were crushed and shocked. As if that shock was not enough, my gynecologist informed me that I was pregnant. Apparently, the "pill" I was using did not work. Our first year of marriage with the draft and my pregnancy was difficult.

The early morning of August 29, 1967, my darling husband, my mother-in-law, and I went to the Greyhound station in Bakersfield and saw Jack off to the Army. The ride home was daunting. I was alone and scared. The thought that Jack could serve and not return was overwhelming.

I had to find a job and take care of Jack's mother. There was just one hitch. I was pregnant. I found a job at the Pepsi Cola Company. The owner, a former Army officer, hired me. I worked hard for him because he was so good to me.

My experience as an Army wife was not so bad until a conversation I had with my doctor's staff: "Yes, I am an Army wife." Right away, the bookkeeper took me aside and said, "You will have to pay $50 each time you come in because you are military." My job did not pay much. With rent and other expenses, the $50 may as well have been $1,000. I was now treated worse than a welfare patient. I was shocked, mad, humiliated. Still, I knew I needed a good doctor for the baby, so I took the looks, the attitude, and paid as I could. However, I gave up our apartment and moved in with my mother-in-law.

Meanwhile, Jack was at Fort Ord. Much to our surprise and gratitude, he was chosen to serve as a chaplain's assistant. He was assigned to the United States Army Chaplain's School at Fort Hamilton, New York. At Christmas, Jack got leave and came home for two weeks. Since he left, we'd had two weekends together in Monterey and the two weeks at Christmas. That is how he got to see me grow with our child, but he was unable to share in the experience. I missed his loving support.

As I found out, military wives were treated pretty badly in civilian life. Many petitioned for a safe haven. The Army took a brave step and created a "Waiting Wives Base" in Salina, Kansas. The women and children of the men fighting over in

Vietnam and Thailand were now safe. Back in New York, the final choice for the chaplain's assistant position in Kansas came down to the two men with pregnant wives. I was further along in my pregnancy, so Jack got the job. When our baby, Christine, was born, we called her our "lucky charm."

Christine and I arrived in Wichita, Kansas. We were met by Jack who drove us to our new home in Salina. It was old Air Force housing with no curtains (just blinds) and no furniture. The Army gave us some old furniture, including a horse hair couch. It was very itchy.

Our introduction to civilian treatment came quickly. We needed a bed and other things for our daughter. We went to the Montgomery Ward store and bought everything on credit. The delivery was supposed to be the next day. The next day, no delivery. We called the store and were told there would be no delivery because we had not lived in the area long enough. We also wanted to buy a television on a two-year contract. We bought the television, but it had to be on a one-year contract. We were military. Our car had California plates. Imagine the looks we got driving down the street.

One of the officer's wives sold us her used crib for $5. She also gave us boxes of cute girl clothes from her three girls. Christine had clothes for years. We had a wonderful group of women and students who helped out at church. We started a youth program with two students. By the time we left, the program had sixty students. We loved the military kids. They were wonderful.

Jack befriended the manager of the commissary's meat department. We purchased day-old meats for three to five dollars a box. We ate steak, roast, chicken. Once, our checkbook got down to thirty-seven cents, but our little girl got the food she needed. The infirmary had two doctors, one who was a kidney specialist. He was angry to be pulled from his research. Our dentists were great, though. They were the only good part of the medical team.

A wonderful member of our chapel, a colonel's wife, and her daughter babysat while I taught the Sunday School high school class. The colonel's wife told me to leave Christine with her for three hours once a week, so I could nap, wash my hair, shop, have some free time. I loved her even though I was intimidated because she was so high up on the military social ladder.

Jack was discharged, August 1970. When we returned home, we went back to our old jobs for a few months. Then, Jack and I loaded our car and trailer. We were off to the University of California, Irvine, where Jack finished his undergraduate and graduate studies.

Five years after we were married, we finally began life as a regular couple. We figure the military put us three years behind most people our age. We also came back to a society that did not care about serving our country with honor. No one ever gave Jack a pat on the back or said, "Thank you." Yes, the unpopular war and the draft did happen. However, being drafted did not mean service without honor or love of country. Young men went and never blinked an eye.

Approximately twenty years after the end of the Vietnam War, the Vietnam Traveling Memorial Wall made its way to Bakersfield's Hillcrest Mortuary. Jack put on his green 5th Army field jacket for the first time since being discharged and wore it to the memorial. It was the first time he felt he could show he served, the first time someone actually thanked him. I wanted to cry.

About fourteen years ago, I was thrilled to find out that I had a patriot who served in our nation's Revolutionary War. I was thrilled to become a member of the Daughters of the American Revolution and to honor the history of my family. My husband also has a patriot in his lineage. Now, we know why we served with pride in the Vietnam era. It is a family thing called love of "God, home, and country."

"I HATE WAR!"

By Denia Pearson Hubbard
Captain John Oldham Chapter, NSDAR
Grass Valley, California

I hate war! Particularly the Vietnam War! I hated the politics that led to the war. I hated the media for demonizing our solders, and I hated the fact that my youngest brother, Hugh John Pearson, was there. He was only nineteen years old when he went, and he turned twenty-one while he was there.

SP/5 Hugh John Pearson
United States Army

He wrote frequently and tried to reassure us that he was okay. I still have those treasured letters. We sent him packages. He and his fellow soldiers seemed to appreciate them very much. Mother sent homemade goodies and packed them all in popcorn. They loved that too. One thing did not work out too well though.......the avocados she put in a pair of shoes he had asked for and did not try to wear for quite some time. I made him tapes of the records he listened to when he lived with me before being drafted. I always tried to speak on the tapes and never succeeded. I did not want him to hear the tears in my voice.

The unit Hugh was with was supply and transportation. They moved camp frequently to be near the infantry. He always set up a "Club" for the guys. I sent packages for the twelve days of Christmas and was comforted to know they used them all.

Hugh wrote about the weather - hot and dry or wet and muddy - and of the mortar fire into camp at night. All the while, he continued to tell us that he was fine. There was always mortar fire aimed at the convoys as they moved supplies.

Hugh spoke of very few incidents, and only after he came home. He cited one for us, saying we would not understand. The unit was experiencing mortar fire on the convoy. They all dove under their trucks. The man he was face-to-face with under the truck got a bullet through the head and died on the spot. Hugh was right; we couldn't comprehend it.

Hugh Pearson at a supply depot, Vietnam

He made it home without being shot; but, oh my, how he suffered physically and mentally. He contracted a disease called Reiter syndrome, a combination of arthritis, iritis (inflammation of the eye's iris) and urinary tract infections. At that time the Veterans Administration medical facility had no answer or diagnosis. He came north to where I lived to see a new internist who diagnosed it immediately.

I remember we were sitting having a beer and he had taken off his laced-up field boots (the only way he could walk because of the inflammation of his feet and ankles) and had to go to the bathroom.

He crawled to the bathroom! I wept. He got it all, severe iritis, losing most of his vision in both eyes. He even got the heart problems that affect only ten percent of the Vietnam veterans. He had an aortic valve replacement and recently, another pacemaker. How he suffered. We all did. Then came the mental problems. He was jittery. He spooked at the slightest movement or sound and couldn't settle down. There was too much noise in his head. He drank too much.

My oldest brother was a mechanic. Hugh went to work for him. They came up with the idea that they could race cars, and we all enthusiasticly supported that idea. One of them built the engines and the other drove. I asked Hugh how he could be such a fearless driver and he said there are no mines on the track. He had driven a jeep in front of the convoys as fast as he could to explode the mines in the road before the convoy passed over.

Racing was a reprieve for all of us and a focus for him until he was injured and could no longer race. Alcohol took over his life. The family finally confronted him and he left with our parents for a clinic in Santa Barbara. Fortunately it worked and he worked to stay on the wagon. He did it! He became a successful developer and builder with the help of his mentor, friends and family. His success was yet another focus that helped quiet his mind. Hugh worked through his physical pain and still is working through his pain.

I hate war!

THE DRAFT DEFERMENT

By Carol Oakley Jackson
State Regent, CSSDAR
Malibu Chapter, NSDAR
Malibu, California

If it hadn't been for the Vietnam War, I would not be living in California. I was an early baby boomer, and the Vietnam War was the focus of my last two years of high school, my four years of college, and all the years of my first marriage.

Carol Oakley, 1969

Maintaining a draft deferment was the top topic of conversation among young men, their girlfriends, and their mothers. For some, the discussion was on dodging the draft altogether. It was a part of any life decision. One of the problems was that the rules were changed frequently. For a time, there were absolute deferments for married men and for men enrolled in college.

Soon, the marriage deferment for men without children came into question. In 1965, that deferment was taken away very suddenly. One of my friends sent out her wedding invitations only to discover that the "big day" was set for the weekend after the marriage deferment was to end. We were oddly proud of the couple's decision to go forward regardless of the consequences. The church wedding went off as planned, draft consequences notwithstanding. We later learned that the couple had been married by a justice of the peace the week before.

The rules changed again on Monday, December 1, 1969, when the first draft lottery occurred. I remember all of us sitting glued to the black-and-white television in the sorority house. The lottery was a drawing to select the first men to be drafted. For the unlucky, this was most likely a ticket to a strange and foreign place where soldiers were dying in increasingly significant numbers. The telecast of the lottery was viewed by a huge audience all across the country. It was almost like the day that Neil Armstrong had walked on the moon just a few months earlier. This one was personal, however, and many were nervous, even scared.

The regularly scheduled program had been preempted. As the ceremony of drawing the capsules containing birthdays began, the announcer introduced the lottery in hushed tones, much like a golf tournament. The days of the year, including February 29th, were represented by the numbers one through 366, written on slips of paper. The slips of paper were placed in separate, blue plastic capsules that were dumped unceremoniously into a deep glass jar. Capsules were drawn from the jar, one at a time. The order in which the numbers were drawn determined the order in which draft-eligible men would be drafted.

It was a life-changing moment. We knew the dates we were listening for, whether we had a brother or were engaged, pinned, lavaliered, or simply dating. I was lavaliered to a "February 11," who became a number 150. He was comfortably 2-S, deferred because of collegiate study and planning to continue on to graduate school. For the time being, there were few worries. Shortly, we were pinned.

I graduated three weeks after the incident at Kent State. My pin man and I were married the next week, and he graduated from college the following year. It was 1971, and he was applying to graduate school when the rules changed once again. Now, there would be no deferment for graduate school. My husband would be 1-A, available for unrestricted military service.

For that year, 1971, the Indiana Selective Service System announced that it was drafting up to number 151. Grad school suddenly became unlikely. My husband applied anyway. He also began the rigorous application for Navy Officer Candidate School. In time, he was accepted for both. He chose Navy OCS, largely because of the looming draft. He was to report to Newport, Rhode Island, the first week of January 1972. On New Year's Eve, as he was packing to leave, the Indiana Selective Service announced that it had drafted to number 149. He would not have been drafted after all.

He was commissioned five months later in May 1972. We were sent to Navy Supply Corps School in Athens, Georgia. In late October of that year, we watched Henry Kissinger stand before the television cameras and state, "Peace is at hand." Shortly after that, we learned that he would be stationed in San Diego at 32nd Street Naval Station. After spending a snowy Thanksgiving in Indiana, we traveled to beautiful Southern California.

It turns out that soon after his three-year active duty was completed, my husband and I parted ways. But then I met Jerry Jackson, and the rest is history.

In 1995, Jerry and I traveled to Vietnam. We were there for three weeks, traveling from Hanoi to Saigon (Ho Chi Minh City). He had been a war correspondent there in 1965 and 1966, and he was glad to visit the places he had lived and worked. I was glad to visit the country that had changed so many lives, including mine.

"THANK GOD, MY DAD CAME HOME"

By Debra Parent Jamison
Honorary State Regent, CSSDAR
Kaweah Chapter, NSDAR
Visalia, California

It was one of greatest honors of my life to be able to recognize my father for his service during the Vietnam conflict, the evening the California State Society kicked off its partnership with the United States of America Vietnam War Commemoration at the 105th California State Conference. The script for the evening was as follows:

Many of our members present this evening know that I am the child of a Vietnam Veteran, and you've heard me speak about the hardships encountered by military families when either Mom or Dad is deployed overseas. In my family, I don't think there ever was a time where we did not know what patriotism was or what it truly meant to be an American. We were just raised that way and we were military kids. My sisters and I always understood the service our dad was performing for the United States of America was very important service. Although my sisters and I were sometimes sad to be moving to a new military base and leaving our friends behind, we were always very proud of what our dad did for a living and we thought he looked pretty spiffy in his uniforms.

Our dad was career Navy; joining in 1956 and retiring in 1976 as a Master Chief. During the last years of the Vietnam War, he served on the USS Oriskany, "The Mighty O," an Essex-class aircraft carrier that now lies at the bottom of the ocean off the coast of Florida where it serves as an artificial reef for sea life. My dad served four tours of duty overseas with Attack Squadron 215 during the Vietnam War, and was away from home 35 of 45 months between 1970 and 1974. His duties aboard ship included Maintenance Material CPO, Career Counselor, Electronics Division Supervisor, and Master Chief of the Command. He ended his military career in 1976 as Assistant Officer in Charge of the Naval Training Detachment at Naval Air Station, Lemoore, California, and work for the Navy as a civil servant. He ended up traveling all over the world as one of a small group of men who repaired computerized radar on aircraft carriers.

Honorary State Regent Debra Parent Jamison
with her father, Charles F. Parent, United States Navy, Ret.
Opening Night of the 105th California Society State Conference,
Daughters of the American Revolution
March 7, 2013

During my dad's military career and after, my parents both were great role models for volunteerism and helping others. During the time when my folks were starting out in the Navy, most young military families really struggled to make ends meet, just like they do today. My parents frequently helped other families who were in great need, even though our family was experiencing some of the same struggles. My sisters will attest to the fact that many times over the years we have watched our dad give someone in distress the last dollar in his wallet. As you can guess, watching my parents' care for others has no doubt influenced my love of volunteerism.

Few of us are rarely given opportunities to publicly thank our loved ones for the support they give us, and for the amazing things they accomplish. It is the greatest honor tonight to give a State Regent's Special Commendation to Charles F. Parent, my favorite Vietnam Veteran and my dad, for his exemplary military service; and especially for his service during the Vietnam War.

As I shared my dad's Vietnam service with the Opening Night assembly, I just kept thinking, "Thank God, my dad came home." Accompanying this thought was the memory of many of my high school classmates whose fathers were either prisoners during the war or were missing in action. I'll never forget the day a friend was called to the principal's office where she found her mother waiting to take her home to tell her that her father was missing in action and presumed deceased. He was never found. Thank God, my dad came home.

NO SOLDIER LEFT BEHIND

By Marge Eytchison Janlois
Mt. Diablo Chapter, NSDAR
Danville, California

In February 1965, the Vietnam War began in earnest. Previously, the American soldiers had been fighting the Viet Cong guerillas in South Vietnam, but they were soon faced by an even greater force. American intelligence determined that the North Vietnamese were sending thousands of troops down the Ho Chi Minh Trail into Cambodia where they knew they were safe from any confrontation with Americans. They then began crossing ten miles into the highlands of South Vietnam to make a base camp in the valley of Ia Drang for the beginning of an assault on the south.

Because of the very difficult terrain, the only access for American troops was by helicopter. The 1st Cavalry with their sixteen Huey helicopters literally became the lifeline for the troops who were sent into the valley. As they were landing troops, the helicopters came under fire. They soon realized they were surrounded by North Vietnamese soldiers. Thus began a thirty-five-day battle which became the bloodiest battle of the entire war.

The commander of the battalion, Colonel Hal Moore, now a retired general, wrote an account of that terrible battle in a best-selling book titled, *We Were Soldiers Once-and Young*. Colonel Moore wrote that he feared this was going to become a repetition of Custer's Last Stand. He contacted headquarters with the code word, "Broken Arrow," meaning, "We are surrounded." He called for air support, but the planes were unable to see through the dense canopy of the jungle to select their targets. They dropped bombs and napalm but were limited because of fear of killing innocent tribal villagers. Ia Drang became known as The Valley of Death. Three hundred fifty American soldiers and 1,235 North Vietnamese died there.

In their Huey helicopter 808, my brother-in-law, Chief Warrant Officer Don Phelps and his three-man crew flew 125 missions into the valley, taking reinforcements, ammunition, and supplies, then flying out with the dead and wounded. Under heavy fire on one mission, he was ordered to leave, but he refused to leave without the wounded. For his heroism, he was awarded the Distinguished Flying Cross. Their last flight was with supplies for the troops in the Northern Highlands. Headquarters lost contact with them, and they disappeared into the jungle. A four-day aerial search failed to find any trace of them. They were then declared Missing in Action. Nothing more was known about the fate of Huey 808 for forty-four years.

On December 28,1965, my younger sister, Dee, received a telegram informing her that her beloved husband, CWO Don Phelps, 28, pilot of a Huey helicopter, had been shot down and lost in the jungle in Vietnam. In spite of his frequent absences in the line of duty, he was a devoted husband and loving father to their four children, ages three to seven years. Devastated, Dee bravely began devoting her life to maintaining a loving and stable home for them without their father. The boys were super athletes, and Dee rarely missed a football or baseball game. Fortunately, our parents lived close by to give them support. The boys' beloved grandfather, "Pop," an avid outdoorsman, took the boys hunting and fishing. Lori, the youngest, loved music and dancing, baking cookies with her grandmother, and keeping up with her three older brothers. They all finished high school and college, married, and now have families of their own.

For decades after the war, family groups and comrades in arms lobbied the United States and Vietnamese governments to search for the crash site of Huey 808. In 2009 the group found an elderly man in a small Montagnard village who showed them an award he had received in 1965 for shooting down an American helicopter. Two villagers led them through the jungle to the very few remains of the helicopter. The helicopter had been scavenged, but enough remained to identify it as Huey 808. The searchers found fragments of bones and teeth, and one ID tag. The remains were sent to the military forensic laboratory in Hawaii. Forty-four years had gone by, but with DNA testing, the lab was able to positively identify all four of the missing crew.

Don's two eldest sons, Ron and Jeff, now grown men, flew to Hawaii to accompany their father's coffin home. As they disembarked, all of the passengers on the commercial United flight remained in their seats until the sons and the flag-draped coffin were on the tarmac. They were met by a military honor guard and a very tearful mother, brother Don, and sister Lori. Lori, the youngest, sobbed as she caressed the casket of the father she had never known. Ron embraced his mother and said to her, "Mom, we have brought him home."

On the route from the airport to the church where the memorial service was held, and then again from the church across the city to the veterans cemetery of Boise, many cars had their lights on, and many hundreds of people stopped their activities and stood attentively as the procession passed by. Military personnel along the way saluted the coffin in respect to a fallen soldier. The funeral procession to the cemetery was led by a group called the Patriot Guard Riders, mounted on thirty Harley motorcycles with American flags flying.

The day of Don's burial, on what would have been his seventy-second birthday, the flags in the state of Idaho were flown at half mast. He was buried in the veterans cemetery overlooking the Boise Valley on land adjacent to Boise's Dry Creek Cemetery. Both cemeteries occupy land homesteaded by our great-grandfather, Thomas Breshears, and his wife, Nancy. They traveled from Missouri in a covered wagon. They had ten children, five of whom died in childhood. Those children were the first to be buried in the Dry Creek Cemetery.

At the funeral service, the governor of Idaho gave a moving tribute to Don and those who had served with him. Don was honored with a beautiful, full military service, a rifle salute, the National Guard Pipers and a Missing Man flyover. Many members of our two families came together from all over the United States, as did two Medal of Honor recipients who had served with Don in Vietnam. It was an exremely tearful, emotional day for all.

Don's brother-in-law, retired Vice Admiral Ron Eytchison, concluded his eulogy with these beautiful words, "After forty-four years, Don is home to be laid to rest in the shadows of the Idaho mountains. Welcome home. Well done, soldier. Be thou at peace."

THE WAITING GAME

By Victoria Kendig
Captain Henry Sweetser Chapter, NSDAR
Santa Maria, California

As I sat at the gravesite of my dear college friend's husband in 1968 and heard taps played, all I could do was weep for the lost life and for my friend. It was absolutely one of the saddest days of my life. This lovely young woman had been deprived of her life's mate, a man full of promise, who was a casualty of the fierce Vietnam Tet Offensive in February 1968. He was my college friend as well as my husband's friend.

Loren Kendig flying in Vietnam

As we laid our friend to rest, my own husband, Loren, was still fighting in Vietnam and had just come through that same awful Tet Offensive. He had been in country about two months as a helicopter pilot when the North Vietnamese Army and the Viet Cong launched their shocking military operation all over South Vietnam. Loren was uninjured but physically and mentally exhausted after living in his chopper for thirteen days. During that time, he experienced very little sleep while ferrying troops to and from various battlefields, and occasionally evacuating the battle's wounded. The pilots and crews had to stay with their aircraft around the clock in case they were needed for an urgent mission, or in the event the enemy hit American airfields with rockets or mortars.

It was back in the United States at our friend's funeral that I began to realize what war truly meant to the families at home. It struck me to the very core. I could relate to those colonial wives who said goodbye as their husbands marched off to fight the British, and those who endured the War of 1812, the Civil War, World Wars I and II, and the Korean War. Vietnam was our generation's war.

Vicky Kendig pinning warrant officer's bars on Loren's uniform, 1967

We sent Loren off to war just before Christmas, 1967. We had high hopes that he could help the Vietnamese people in their fight against communism - in a faraway country we'd barely heard of and, before the outbreak of combat, certainly couldn't locate on a map.

That day at the funeral, my confidence suddenly and completely vanished. A primal fear that Loren would never make it home replaced my previously cocky attitude that all would be well in spite of everything. That is when I really began to pray.

During Loren's year in Vietnam, I had a love-hate relationship with the media. Each day after teaching school, I would rush home to scan the newspaper and catch a glimpse on television of what was happening in that faraway and exotic place. I would study the Vietnam map my husband sent me to try to pinpoint how close to his airfield at Soc Trang the newest fighting had erupted.

I would yell and turn off the television when the reports showed a helicopter crashing. On the other hand, when the newscasts showed helicopters saving lives, I would cry with joy that men and women - both American and South Vietnamese - would be able to return to their families, thanks to the crews and the skilled pilots who flew the choppers.

Though television was important to me, the mail was my personal lifeline to Loren. We wrote each other every day and sent an audio tape almost every week.

Sometimes Loren's letters would arrive in such a jumbled chronology that they wouldn't make sense. He would refer to an important incident as if I should know about it. A few days later, I'd get the original explanatory letter written days before the other one. This situation often proved to be funny, but other times not. Once I received a tape in which Loren said he hoped I wasn't too upset on learning of his helicopter crash. A flash of panic hit. Then I realized that, of course, he was okay. A few days later, the letter that had been written earlier arrived, explaining his accident in detail. That brief, heart-stopping moment was just one example of how news often was, and is to this day, incorrectly perceived by families on the home front.

Despite some of those glitches, it's impossible to give the postal service enough credit for the job they did for service members and families during the war. Postage from Vietnam was free for the military, and the letters and packages usually arrived in a timely manner.

Loren's mom and I would bake a bunch of goodies every week and mail them to him to share with his buddies. He was one popular warrant officer! Once in a while, though, the contents would be green with mold when they finally reached their destination.

Another group of people who were a blessing for me and other military families at home were the ham radio operators. I would receive calls at all hours, day and night, from a ham operator asking if I would stand by for a call from my husband.

You could hear the pride and excitement in the operators' voices as they put the call through.

A real morale-booster anticipated by both Loren and me was the week-long R & R in Hawaii. Just to be able to hold each other during that short time seemed like heaven. At the end of the week, I joined the long line of wives who watched and sobbed as their husbands loaded onto planes heading back to the war zone.

Fast forward forty-five years to 2013. Loren and I were in Angel Fire, New Mexico, and decided to visit the Vietnam Veterans Memorial. It sits on a wind-swept mountain overlooking the peaceful Moreno Valley. What we discovered there surprised and delighted us. On display in the memorial gardens is a UH-1 Huey that Loren occasionally flew in Vietnam. It was from his unit, the 121st Assault Helicopter Company. That chopper really represents the war to me. It carried my husband safely through some extremely dangerous battles. For that, I am eternally grateful.

I feel so blessed that Loren returned to us, and that we have both lived to see two children and four grandchildren grow. I grieve for those many wives, children, parents, and siblings who never saw their military loved ones on earth again.

I'm also proud of my husband, who did his best to save lives while he served. He was honored with the Distinguished Flying Cross - the highest aviation award for an Army aviator next to the Medal of Honor - for his bravery in an operation that resupplied ammunition and food to troops pinned down by enemy fire. Many soldiers eventually made it home to their families because of the unselfish actions of Loren and his crew.

THE VIEW FROM GERMANY

By Sally Knutson
Captain John Oldham Chapter, NSDAR
Grass Valley, California

I spent the 1960's in Gelnhausen, Germany, teaching dependent children for the Department of Defense. The 3rd Armored Division, Central Command B (CCB) was stationed in Gelnhausen. This base was strategically located in the Fulda Gap, the historic invasion and retreat route of Napoleon, and the natural channel from central Germany to the east.

When the Russians built the Berlin Wall in 1961, the United States feared an invasion from the Union of Soviet Socialist Republics (USSR). It was thought that a ground invasion of western Europe would come through the Fulda Gap. The men in Gelnhausen were put on 24-hour alert after the Bay of Pigs incident in Cuba. Since we made a GS rating equivalent to that of an officer, we had use of the Officers' Club. This made for a lot of togetherness between the teachers and the officers. Officers could not leave post, and we were young and on hand. We got to know these young men very well. Many of them were first and second lieutenants. Several had graduated from West Point and were on their first overseas assignment.

The Kennedy assassination in 1963 tightened things even more. We started to see some of our officers leave for Vietnam with new assignments. The pilots were the first to go. These young men were eager to get to Vietnam and into combat. They were well trained, and many of them were headed for Army careers. Their excitement was transmitted to us, and we were happy that they were happy.

We all felt going to Vietnam to repel the Communists was the right thing to do. As Americans, we felt it was our duty to defeat Communism anywhere it showed its ugly head.

Almost all of the officers I knew and partied with had a tour in Vietnam. One very, very good friend was killed. Another had his legs injured so badly they didn't think he would ever walk again. Several came home and have not been the same men who went to Vietnam. Our very good friend and Post Commander, Colonel Woodward, became General Woodword in Vietnam. Generals Colin Powell and Creighton Abrams were former CCB, Gelnhausen residents.

I came home to California in 1968 and met my husband-to-be, Roger Knutson. Roger had been in the Army but was a civilian now with the heart of a pacifist. He was as anti-war and anti-Vietnam as I was pro-Vietnam. He loved the anti-war rallies. I hated them. We really didn't talk about it too much, but I was receiving mail from wives of some of the fellows from Gelnhausen who were in Vietnam. Several of the wives stopped to visit me on their way to Hawaii to see their husbands. Roger was always very polite and cordial, but I knew he didn't feel very sympathetic.

As the war continued and things in Vietnam got worse instead of better, I have to admit I, too, grew to hate the war and wondered why we were wasting our good men over there. Many of my good friends retired with high military ranks, but I wonder if they would have been just as successful if they had not served in the Vietnam War.

THE IMPACT AFTER THE WAR

By Adele Lancaster
State Corresponding Secretary, CSSDAR
Santa Margarita Chapter, NSDAR
Oceanside, California

From 1961 to 1965, I was a student attending a small college in San Diego. Unlike so many students on larger campuses throughout the country, I was mostly isolated from the events of the time. Our residence had no television, so we were not exposed to the "war brought into the living room." I never burned my bra or joined with protestors. Rather, my primary exposure was through active involvement at a large church in San Diego. Its youth group served three primary populations: college age, military, and young working men and women. Almost every Sunday evening, we were saying good-bye - standing in a circle, arms around each other singing, "Blessed be the Tie that Binds" - to another member of our group who was being sent overseas. These were bitter-sweet times. We knew what they faced but were relieved that they faced the foe from aboard ships. We also knew that with their leaving, other friends would be returning. Our role was to support those who served.

When I left college and began working as a teacher, I still had no television, but I did have a newspaper. I became much more aware, noticing how often a friend from high school serving with the 2nd platoon, Alpha Company was quoted regarding fierce fighting. I also became much more aware of the anti-war efforts, the divide being fostered by Jane Fonda and others. When I met and married my husband, who had three family members who had or were serving in the war, I began to realize the extremely negative impact the actions of the protestors were having on those men and their families. Then, in 1967, the war came home with the death of a high school friend who was serving in Vietnam as a helicopter pilot.

The real impact of the Vietnam War on my life, though, was most profound after the war. Camp Pendleton became a receiving station for Vietnamese refugees coming from the war-torn country immediately after the fall of Saigon. A call was put out to San Diego residents to serve as foster parents to unaccompanied teens. All seven of our foster children had been separated from their families, with parents left behind in Vietnam after having done everything possible to get their children out of the country. One family had been preparing for years for their daughter to join her older brother in France where he attended college. The fall came first. Another daughter's father had her board a ship in the Saigon harbor during military action, not realizing the ship was leaving port. A third daughter, eleven years of age, traveled with an older brother; but had herself designated, "no family," so she could be placed alone with a family. In the frantic last-minute chaos of a city under siege, a fourth daughter, age twelve, was running onto the airbase with older siblings in hopes they would all leave the city together. They were separated when the gates were slammed shut. As she was rushed onto an aircraft ready for takeoff, her siblings were left behind. They were finally able to get to the United States twenty years later.

Our two boys hid from the Viet Cong in small boats in people's backyards until their parents could sneak them onto the airbase at the beginning of the end. Our last daughter is considered a "boat person." Her escape came nearly four years after the communist takeover through secret deals her mother made with members of black market groups offering safe transport for cash and jewels. Her experiences included a boat so crowded there was no room to move, sleeping spoon-fashion with strangers, no area for "relieving" oneself, and a small daily portion of rice. Conditions were not much better in the Malaysian refugee camps where it took nearly a year to get her cleared to come to the United States.

These children grew to become productive, contributing, American citizens, cognizant of the vast opportunities for work and education found here. Today they are raising children of their own. Though they have returned to Vietnam to visit family, they proudly call America "Home Sweet Home." And, we are still proud to call them ours.

From my perspective, they are the ones with remarkable stories to tell.

Vietnamese Children of Tom and Adele Lancaster

Bich Nguyen

Huo Nguyen

Anh Nguyen

Van Vu

Cac Nguyen

KimLan Nguyen

Cuong Nguyen

A DAILY REMEMBRANCE

By June Lazich
Irvine Ranch Chapter, NSDAR
Irvine, California

Everyday, Vietnam War memories remain vivid in my thoughts and heart. I only have to look at the American flag flying in my backyard to remember what took place. There was rioting in the streets and prayers in the homes of those who had sons and loved ones serving during the conflict. Total controversy about whether or not we needed to be there flooded the newspapers. Are we not the world's "Sweet Land of Liberty?" Are we to sit still and do nothing when we see injustice in the world? Over time we have kept the faith with the blood of our dearest and best, who gave their lives for freedom.

So it was in this conflict. I was a mother of three girls, two in high school and one under ten years old. I was working the Bob's Big Boy in Whittier, California, as the night head waitress. The restaurant was well known as the teen/college hangout, and students patrolled Whittier Boulevard every weekend.

The year was 1968 and Jim, our night head cook, was leaving soon to join the Army. Jim and I usually had dinner together while we discussed problems and schedules. He planned to be an engineer and took classes daily while working nights. We shared a love of classical music, our country, and - as our birthdays were a few days apart - the company birthday cake made for personnel. We often talked about my joining the Daughters of the American Revolution. I knew I was eligible with many patriots in my lineage. I was also elibigle for the Mayflower Society.

Before Jim left for training, another cook named John returned from his first tour of Vietnam. He had only a few weeks at home, before returning for his second tour. I promised to write to him, and we all sent cookies and letters to cheer him up. His description of the brutality and horror there, then people calling him names when he returned home, kept him wondering why he was there. His morale was shaken. He would mail half-finished letters because combat was continuous. John was in the 1st Cavalry and returned safely, spending his last year of service in Germany.

However, Jim had a short training period and left quickly. He came to see me just before he left, and told me he probably would not return. He said he was not a soldier, but he was proud to serve his country and would do his best, especially for me.

In two months, we received word that Jim was missing in action. A month later, his body was sent home to be buried. His parents buried him in Rose Hills Memorial Park's Oriental Section. "Since he died for them," they said. I could not go to Jim's funeral, but I have visited his grave and the Vietnam Wall where his name is enshrined forever. Whenever I look at the ornament atop our flag, I see Jim's face. I thank him for his love of country and for his sacrifice.

It was years later that I presented General James B. Davis (former NATO commander) with the DAR Medal of Honor. At that time, I couldn't help but think of James Alan Davis, the Big Boy's head cook. Each day, as I say the Pledge of Allegiance to the Flag of the United States in my yard, I remember those I knew - and those from whom I am descended - who have served and died:

Afghanistan - USMC: Lance Cpl. Donald Hogan

Vietnam - USA: James Davis, John Douglas, Green Beret Robert LaGanke

Korea - USA: Wayne Knesebeck, Charles Getts

WWII - USA: Robert Butara; Dwight Brainard (my father); Sam Lam, Albert Lam, Michael Lam (my uncles); Robert Jones; Jack Toney, Glen Toney, Gene Toney

USN: Enoch Brainard and William Lam (my uncles); Perry Geller (my cousin), Winnie Johnson Geller

USMC: Henry Geller and James Brainard (my cousins), Juanita Toney

Civil War - USA: Enoch S. Brainard (my grandfather)

War of 1812 - USA: Silas Brainard (my great-grandfather)

Revolutionary War - Enoch Brainard, Ichabod Rogers, Edward Tryon, William Southworth, Nathan Southworth, Abijah Brainard, Josiah Jr., and Josiah Sr. Brainard.

May we always remember that freedom is not free.

THE WHIRLWIND ROMANCE

By Shirley Muir-Mathews
Western Shores Chapter, NSDAR
Long Beach, California

It was the summer of 1964. I lived with my mother and sister in a small house in Fullerton, California. My mother sent me on an errand next door to our neighbor Betty's house. I barged into her house, as was my custom, but I pulled up short. She had a visitor I had never seen before. He was a Marine from Camp Pendlton. I didn't realize it at the time because he was in civilian clothes.

He was a friend of her family from back east, a Corporal Douglas Wood. I remember thinking that he was very handsome and powerful. I quickly concluded my business and retreated home.

I couldn't stop thinking about that guy next door, and I soon made up an excuse to return to Betty's house. Doug and I struck up an immediate friendship. I didn't know if our friendship would be an issue because my father was a career Navy man. You know how the different services feel about each other.

Shirley Muir

After a whirlwind courtship, we eloped. A short time later Doug was deployed back to Vietnam. This was his second deployment, but this time it was for a full combat beach landing, the first of the Vietnam Conflict.

While on his way to Vietnam, Doug wrote to me and requested a photo to carry with him. I sent the photo you see, here, and Doug carried it with him to every camp and foxhole. Once, there was a bunkhouse fire. When the fire was extinguished and they were able to return, he found my picture unharmed.

There were just a few drops of water on it and Doug said he imagined that I was crying.

Doug requested that I move in with his mother so he would feel I was safe and need not worry about me. Not wanting him to worry, I did my part. I packed myself up and boarded a plane to Indiana.

The problem was, I had never met any of his family. I didn't even know how I was going to find his folks at the airport. I had been given an old picture of them, but it wasn't very clear. As it turned out, they found me and welcomed me with hugs and kisses. They took me in as one of their own daughters. For some reason, I had not worried for one moment that they would.

I was still in high school, so I needed to register before school started. I was a Navy brat and a world traveler, but I had never lived in a landlocked, snowy place. I didn't know how to walk on the white stuff. Not having the right clothing and shoes led to many falls, bruises, soakings, and nearly frostbitten digits. There were also stares and whispers from other students. I was dressed like a California girl and looked quite out of place. It was embarrassing.

Doug's mother and I would sit in front of the television every evening, fixated on the news from Vietnam. We would stare intently at the screen, hoping to catch a glimpse of Doug. The worry was palapable.

After thirteen months, my husband came home. It was just in time. I was beginning to forget what he looked like. From the time we met, fell in love, got married and his deployment, was a mere three months. I waited at the house with his mother and siblings for his arrival. His brother had driven to the airport to retrieve him. Would I recognize him? Would I even like him? Here I was, married to a stranger! I watched from the screen door as the car pulled up. As the car door opened, I escaped his mother's house. The next thing I remember was being in his crushing arms. After a few seconds we separated. I looked at him and there he was, Sergeant Douglas Wood. He was still a handsome and powerful man, although maybe a little older in the eyes. I fell in love all over again.

MY EXPERIENCE AS A STEWARDESS

By Barbara McMahon
State Organizing Secretary, CSSDAR
Sierra Amador Chapter, NSDAR
Jackson, California

I had goals long before I heard of bucket lists. Graduate from college - check, June 1967.

See the world - check. When I became a stewardess for Trans International Airlines in January 1968, it was the best way I knew to see the world. TIA was a charter airline operating out of Oakland, California. It was a dream job for a young, single woman ready to see as much of the world as possible on someone else's dime and, I actually got paid for it!

The war in Vietnam was escalating. The majority of the flights I was assigned to were MAC (Military Airlift Command), flying troops into and out of Vietnam. We were issued Department of Defense cards identifying us with the rank of lieutenant - in case we were captured by the enemy we would be treated as officers. That was unexpected.

A typical flight, " 'round the horn," as we called it, departed from Travis Air Force Base. Flights usually departed at some awfully early hour like 7:00 a.m. That meant we had to leave home around 4:00 a.m. to get there in time to check out the aircraft before the troops boarded. Jetways weren't available, so we used stairs from the tarmac to the plane. Military regulations required one stewardess to stand at the base of the stairs, one at the door.

The trips over were always full, with the soldiers demonstrating a mixture of anticipation, anxiety, comic relief, and somber reflection. It was a long flight for the troops, but the airline crew only flew one segment at a time. When the plane landed to refuel at Honolulu, the crews were changed. A new crew flew to either Wake Island or Clark Air Force Base, the Philippines, on the next leg.

After a layover that lasted anywhere between twelve hours and four days, our crew would pick up another plane for that next leg to either Wake or Clark. That was a long stretch. We had a couple of meal services and visited with the men, who, for the most part, were around the same age as the stewardesses. We did not talk about war, or about what they were facing. We talked about where they were from, the girl they left behind, what movies they'd seen, and how we became stewardesses.

The final leg was into and out of Vietnam. No layovers there. After landing and the soldiers disembarking, the plane would be refueled. If we had soldiers departing "Nam" on the outbound flight, the stewardesses would clean the aircraft between those deplaning and those coming on board. Vietnam nationals were not allowed on or near the planes.

War zones aren't like commercial airports. There wasn't any air conditioning while on the ground. We didn't get priority, the fighter jets did. And, all the time, there was the worry the enemy would attack, and we wouldn't get our jet out in time.

It was hot and humid in Vietnam. Whether we were in Da Nang, Cam Ranh Bay, or Ben Hoa, a wind always seemed to be blowing. Once, we were on the ground for hours in Da Nang because we couldn't get our jet refueled. The Air Force was flying sorties and all fueling was for the fighter jets. We sat in a protected area near the bunkers and watched the jets take off. It was sort of cool when the afterburners ignited. It was well into the night before our jet was fueled and we could leave. Another time, we circled for what seemed like hours because the base where we were to land was under attack, and they didn't want the enemy to shoot us out of the air.

The hardest station was standing at the base of the stairs in Vietnam, bidding farewell to the very quiet, solemn soldiers filing past as they headed into the unknown. Then there were those leaving as they climbed the stairs to the plane, almost afraid to believe they were actually going home. There was very little talking among them. Some would smile in passing; others avoided eye contact. The saddest part was seeing the aluminum caskets loaded into the belly of the plane. Some trips it seemed the line of silver-colored caskets was never ending. Boys that age should not be going home in caskets. Even I knew that, way back when.

Once the doors closed and the pilot started the engines, all the soldiers seemed to look out the windows. But once we were wheels up, the cheering would have shaken the rafters, if planes had rafters. Those young men were ready to go home!

I wish the homeward flights had been happier for the soldiers. They were definitely glad to be leaving the jungle behind, but most of them had left happiness behind long ago when they first arrived in the war zone. Sleep captured most, as if they knew they were finally completely safe and could sleep as long as they wanted.

We would fly to Yokota Air Base in Japan. Crews would change. Japan was so vibrant after the solemnity and scariness of Vietnam. It was a welcome change for the crews who had layovers until the next plane arrived from "Nam." Sometimes a plane was empty except for the caskets in the belly that we couldn't see but knew were there.

The flight from Yokota went to Anchorage, then back to Travis. The complete trip for a crew was between ten days and three weeks.

The reason military personnel party hard, I think, is for a period of time to forget the horrors of war, the pain of friends and comrades falling in battle, and the futility of so many efforts. Sometimes the crew partied hard, too, to forget what we'd seen.

My thanks to all the men and women who served our country so well in the conflict that was Vietnam.

TWO VIETNAM MEMORIES

By Sharon Meigs
Susan B. Anthony Chapter, NSDAR
Long Beach, California

It was a cold, gray day in January, 1987. Snow was falling as we trudged to Arlington National Cemetery to view the Iwo Jima Memorial. While walking up the drive to the entrance, I noticed a man standing by a pillar. He looked lost. I asked if I could help. He turned toward me and said, "I have to get to the Vietnam War Memorial!" He looked anxious and reached for his wallet. He pulled a piece of paper out of the wallet with a list of names and exclaimed, "These are my friends who didn't make it. I have to get to the Memorial so I can say goodbye to them." By then tears were falling from my eyes, mixing with the melting snowflakes. I was so moved it was hard to speak. I managed to turn him around and point him in the right direction. I instructed him to walk to the end of the drive, cross the Arlington Memorial Bridge, walk past the Lincoln Memorial, and from there he would see the Vietnam Memorial on his left. I will never forget that day. It remains one of the most memorable Vietnam memories of my life.

My other memory is of the entire family driving to McClellan Air Force Base in 1967 to see my older brother, Loren, off for Air Force training. To avoid the draft, he had volunteered to serve four years in the Air Force. The family photograph was taken by a long-time friend in Danville. We stopped at his home for a short visit while on the way to the base. A few hours later, we arrived at the

The Vietnam Memorial, January 1987
Washington, D.C.

base where we had to say our goodbyes. Although we were all emotional, it was the sight of my mother crying as she kissed him goodbye that I will always remember. Loren was stationed at Clark Air Force Base in the Philippines. He served as a mobile communications technician. He made several trips to Vietnam, the longest being for three months.

Three years later, my other brother, George, was drafted into the Army. He was a member of the Old Guard at Fort Meyer, Virginia and served in Honor Guards as the caskets with fallen comrades were removed from airplanes, as well as during burial ceremonies at Arlington National Cemetery.

We were all very relieved when both returned from their time in the service, in one piece. Unfortunately, the Vietnam War had more impact on both than we realized. George found it difficult at first to deal with the anti-war mentality of those he encountered after returning home. Loren discovered years later that his health issues were caused by exposure to Agent Orange. The Vietnam War definitely had an impact on our family that lasted long after the end of the war.

The Meigs Family, 1967
Photo taken in Danville,
California

Left to right: Clara Harris,
Sharon Meigs, Loren Meigs,
Jr., George Meigs, Blenn
Meigs and Loren Meigs, Sr.

TOUGH TREATMENT

By Joy Montgomery
Josefa Higuera Chapter, NSDAR
Livermore, California

I grew up in San Francisco with very mixed signals about the military. Uncle Harold was wounded at the Battle of the Bulge in WWII. As a little girl, I thought I would grow up and marry him. On the other hand, I was warned about men in uniform as if they were in the same category as the "Bogey Man." Supposedly, they were capable of unspecified horrors, and I needed to stay away from them. I was even afraid of policemen and firemen.

In my late teens, members of my church started a group called San Francisco Lutheran Single Adults. At that time, people were being sent to Vietnam, but we were not calling it a war. We were approached by Mrs. Meyers, widow of a Lutheran minister, who asked us to come and socialize with the men and boys who came into the Lutheran Servicemen's Center. The response from the group was completely negative. I couldn't reconcile Christianity and this rejection. Mrs. Meyers and I thought so much alike that she later told me she thought she had acquired a Siamese twin. I couldn't ignore her request for help, but I was terrified being in the same place with people in uniform. I tried to stay in the kitchen, cooking hamburgers. My contact with service personnel at that time was limited to serving hamburgers.

I met some of the best people I've ever known at the center. I had a car. We often drove to Sacramento for pizza at a place we heard about. When someone new would say California was ugly, we'd fill the car and head up to Yosemite for the day. We'd sing in the car. When one soldier whose family owned a dairy farm in Illinois was scheduled to go on a nine month cruise and hadn't had a chance to go home, I found a dairy farm in Sonoma County where the farmer let us wander around for awhile. On another occasion, we rode bikes through Golden Gate Park. It was the first time I ever fit in with a group. To them, I was "one of the guys." We talked about anything and everything.

I was a Sunday School teacher. I sang in the choir. I arranged altar flowers most Saturdays. I was one of the organizers of the San Francisco Lutheran Single Adults. I was dating a deacon. My volunteering at the Lutheran Servicemen's Center ended all of that. I invited the guys from the center to my church. People snubbed them. People snubbed me.

For awhile, my parents were polite and even seemed to like a couple of the guys. Christmas time involved multiple trips each night to the Emporium department store to help the guys pick out gifts for mothers, sisters, nieces, grandmothers, and girlfriends back home. Women from church would call my mother to report who I was spending time with. Even those whose kids who were in my Sunday School class or those who were in the choir with me would start conversations with my mother by saying, "I saw your daughter last night. She was with (pause) a sailor." My mother was ashamed. She screamed at me that they didn't spend all that money sending me to Lutheran school to have me associate with sailors.

I moved away from home. Almost forty years later, the rift within my family with regard to the Vietnam era still emerges at certain times. That discord is just one example of the strong, divisive feelings spawned by the events of the 1960's and 1970's.

SMOKE IN THE CABIN

By Rebecca Baker Moran
El Redondo Chapter, NSDAR
Redondo Beach, California

Smoke or fire in the cabin of an airliner requires rapid emergency response from cabin crew, but it elicits different memories for me of R & R (Rest and Relaxation, Recreation or Recuperation) flights operating in and out of Vietnam during the war. In 1966, Pan American Airways contracted with the United States government to provide the majority of civil airlifts. These included movement of medical supplies, mail, material and personnel across the Pacific in support of our armed forces in Southeast Asia. Flights included MAC charters transporting troops in and out of the war zone for rest and recuperation.

Having been hired as a Pan Am flight attendant based in Los Angeles in 1968, I volunteered over a two-year period as one of the six cabin crew for these flights. Our Boeing 707 aircraft had been reconfigured from the normal first class/economy cabins to an endless sea of seats in rows stretching from the front entry door to the back of the aircraft. The highest-ranking officers occupied seats in the front row opposite the galley and closest to the cockpit.

From September 1969 to August 1970, I flew eight of these eight-day trips to and from Los Angeles with layovers in Honolulu and Guam.

Rebecca Baker Moran
Tan Son Nhut Airport, Saigon

Only after leaving Guam would we learn our destination in Vietnam. It was usually Saigon or Da Nang. These were very long but rewarding days, working five-hour flights each way, to and from Guam. We had less than an hour on the ground to refuel, unload and load troops and baggage, and load our commissary items that had been provided for the round trip. The ground staff performing all these maneuvers were well trained. They landed us safely and got us back in the air as quickly as possible. Only once did we dare ask permission to go into Tan Son Nhut Airport in Saigon to take photos and have our passports stamped.

The mood of the troops was somber as they returned to the war zone from R & R in Hawaii, Tokyo, Australia, or Hong Kong. I was only twenty-two at the time, barely older than many of the servicemen on board. Therefore, I found their "Yes, ma'am" and "No, ma'am" responses a bit awkward. With my Southern upbringing, I did, on occasion, try to explain these responses to some of our many foreign flight attendants who also volunteered for these missions. Of course, we seldom encountered such courtesies on our flights elsewhere in the world.

The troops leaving Vietnam were tired but visibly happy to see six smiling, manicured, white-gloved young women welcoming them on board. Dare I mention that we had already put in a seven-hour workday? However, we were eager to make their trip out of "Nam" a pleasant one. Some wanted to chat with us after the meal service, but most just rested, finally able to relax a little for the first time in months.

The meal served was standard on all our flights: teriyaki steak, potato tots, green peas, salad, rolls, butter, and ice cream for dessert. The main course was frozen solid, and it took quite some doing to thaw it and not overcook the steaks. Immediately after meal service, the cabin filled with so much cigarette smoke that we could not see the opposite end of the aircraft. I had never seen so much smoke in my life and certainly not so dense that we could not see our flying partners. We used the intercom in the galleys to contact one another to avoid trips through the cabin, while holding our breath.

Although smoking was allowed on aircraft at that time, nothing we had seen compared to what we experienced on those charter flights.

As a young woman representing the US flagship carrier Pan Am, it truly was an honor to be part of the war effort, assisting our troops in some small way. We were issued Geneva Convention cards along with cards giving us Air Force officer status in case our planes were attacked. As added bonus, these cards allowed us to shop in the base exchanges at the Guam and Yokota Air Bases. We took full advantage of these opportunities.

In April 1975, Pan Am flew some of the last flights out of Saigon conducting Operation Baby Lift. The airline brought out nearly 3,300 infants and children, the largest number evacuated. Adoptive families were waiting for them in the United States, Europe, and Australia. Flying to Vietnam during the war was one of the most memorable times in my thirty-five-year flying career.

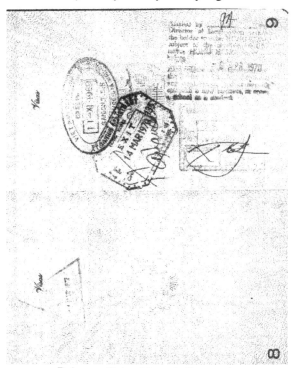

Rebecca Baker Moran's Passport,
stamped at Tan Son Nhut Airport, Saigon

LONG NIGHT AT LANDING ZONE JOY

By Joanne Murphy
Rancho Buena Vista Chapter, NSDAR
Vista, California

In September 1968, my husband, Captain Kevin R. Murphy, United States Army, left for Vietnam. He was headed for the 1st Cavalry Division (Airmobile), 30th Field Artillery. Kevin left me and our two boys, Arthur (age three and one half) and Brendan (age one), in a 1939 cottage in West Palm Beach, Florida.

When Kevin first arrived "in country" (Vietnam), he was assigned to Camp Evans near the Demilitarized Zone (DMZ). His assignment was as a battalion intelligence (S-2) officer calling in firepower from a light aircraft flying low over a battle area. I was quite fearful of the plane's durability as well as of my husband being shot down. My fears were baseless, as after several months he was unscathed.

Captain Kevin R. Murphy, United States Army
Demilitarized Zone, Vietnam

In November 1968, Kevin assumed command of Battery C, 1st Battalion, 30th Artillery. His Battery had six 155mm howitzers. They were the "Big Guns" of the 1/30th. The howitzer fired a variety of projectiles weighing approximately 100 pounds each to a range of 9.2 miles. It was noted for its accuracy and destructive power.

As each day, week, and month pased while Kevin was in Vietnam, I watched the television news in the morning and evening. At that time, the news was delayed a least a day. I received tapes from Kevin as well as letters with news clippings pertaining to the different battles in which his battery was involved. At the time, the 1st Cavalry seemed to be in the thick of it.

Battery C, 1st Battalion, 30th Artillery, Vietnam
One of the six Howitzers is in the background.

Kevin was very good about maintaining contact with the parents of his soldiers, particularly when they first arrived at the battery or received a new position. Kevin shared one or two of the letters with me. One letter from a father mentioned how fortunate his son, Joe, who was newly assigned by Kevin as the C Battery fire directions officer, felt to be a member of the 1st Cavalry Division and particularly C Battery under Kevin's Command. He also mentioned kidding his son that the 1st Air Cavalry was getting all the publicity on television, radio and in the newspaper.

Another letter was from a couple in Sunland, California. They wrote of their gratitude at learning where there son was stationed and what he was assigned to do. They expressed their pride in his accomplishments and their hopes that he would add to the honors and distinctions already earned by the soldiers under Kevin's leadership. They were of Irish descent and were very pleased to know that their son's commanding officer was also of Irish descent. They ended the letter by wishing the 1st Calvary Division health and success, and thanking Kevin for his letter to them. I may be prejudiced, but I think the families with loved ones under Kevin's command fared better than many other family members who received little or no communication from the battle front.

On June 13, 1969, I returned home with the children. Before we entered the house, I grabbed the mail. While cooking dinner, I watched the television news. The news mentioned a 1st Cavalry firefight at "Landing Zone Joy." It sounded fierce! After preparing dinner, feeding the children, bathing them, reading them a story and tucking them into bed, I reached for the mail. The first piece I selected was a letter from Kevin dated June 7, 1969. You cannot imagine my dismay as I read his letter to discover he was no longer at Landing Zone Libby, where he had been moved on May 24, 1969, but that his battery had been airlifted on June 7, 1969, to Landing Zone Joy. I said, "Oh, my God!" I already knew that zone was where, on June 12th, Landing Zone Joy came under heavy mortar, rocket and ground attack. There I sat, not knowing what I could do. I called my parents. My dad, a retired Army colonel, reassured me by saying that if anything had happened to Kevin, I would have already heard. The next day, more reports of the battle were posted:

Battery C was hit by a fierce rocket and mortar barrage followed by a ground attack by 450 North Vietnamese Regular [NVR] troops. Charlie [slang for NVR] blew several holes in the perimeter wire. 50 to 60 NVA at the same time headed for the holes, 1st Cavalry soldiers manning their posts on the berm detonated claymore and fragmentation grenades as they approached...Some NVA... got through the holes but were eventually killed. The next morning when the battle area was surveyed, 17 of the 35 NVR killed were killed inside the perimeter! C Battery had no one killed and 6 wounded, but all not critical.

What a relief that news article gave me. Kevin was awarded a Bronze Star with a "V" (for Valor) for his leadership during the "Landing Zone Joy" battle.

Joanne and Kevin Murphy.

"WE REGRET TO INFORM YOU"

By Carol Lee Olney
Sierra Amador Chapter, NSDAR
Jackson, California

I wasn't yet ten years old when the Vietnam War began, but one memory still stands out after all these years - the role my father had in notifying families when they'd lost a loved one in combat.

Ours was a military house-hold, and my younger siblings and I grew up proud of our parents. Mom was a registered nurse and college instructor. Dad was a lieutenant commander in the United States Navy. Every two to three years, the Navy would shift our father's duty station and assignment, which meant we moved around a lot. The early sixties found us living in Columbus, Georgia, deep in the heart of Dixie, and known affectionately as the "Lowell of the South." Given that our parents were born and raised in New England, and their families had been there for generations, we kids tried

Lieutenant Commander
Grant Lindsey Mitchell
United States Navy

to maintain an awareness of shifting local opinions about the Blues versus the Grays.

My father had command of the Naval Reserve Training Center in Columbus. One of his areas of responsibility was to personally notify local families that a loved one had died in, or as a result of, combat. We were too young to understand why our dad left the house in his service dress uniform; but from his expression, we did know something serious was going on.

Years later, I asked my dad what those mysterious trips were all about. He got quiet for a minute, then he explained that he was making "casualty assistance notification calls" to next of kin on behalf of the United States Government, and that he usually had another officer with him. Given how rural much of the surrounding area was, the two of them often drove for miles to reach the homes of those he had to notify. Arriving unannounced, he truly had to be the last person anyone wanted to see as he walked solemnly up to each house. In most cases he was met with shock and horror.

"On behalf of the Secretary of the Navy, I regret to inform you that _____ died today of_____."

One time, the father of the young seaman who died held a shotgun to his chest as he met my dad at the front door. The father told him not to come any closer because he and his wife did not want to hear what he had to say. Another time, the wife of the fallen officer grabbed the lapels of my dad's uniform jacket and tore them in her grief. While he never knew how the notifications would turn out, one thing he did know was that they would likely be rough.

Regardless of what happened, my father was committed to carrying out his responsibilities. He served as a bridge between the families and their loved ones who served and died overseas, and the men and women of the United States Navy. The Navy is proud of its long line of patriots, fighting since this country's origins for what makes the United States the leader of the free world.

CAPTAIN DAVID OROZCO, USN

By Sandra Deatsch Orozco
Tomo-Kahni Chapter, NSDAR
Tehachapi, California

The story of my husband's involvement in the Vietnam War is a relatively quiet one. Dave Orozco was in pilot training with the United States Navy in Florida for the eighteen months before we were married. We saw each other eighteen days during that time.

We were married on November 3, 1963. Three months later, March 3, 1964, he left North Island Naval Air Station, Coronado, to join his ship in Honolulu. He was attached to his squadron, VS-33, aboard the aircraft carrier USS *Bennington*, designated CVS-20.

Dave flew the Grumman S2-E, a propeller driven, twin-engine plane, designed for anti-submarine warfare. There were no submarines in the waters they sailed, so the squadron was mainly on patrol. Dave got lots of experience with carrier landings. The *Bennington* was not large by modern carrier standards, so the flying was intense, even in a propeller-driven aircraft.

Captain David Anthony Orozco aboard the USS *Bennington*, 1964

The planes were launched by a steam-driven catapult that had a harness attached to the body of the aircraft. The power of the "cat shot" was adjusted to the weight of the plane. Returning to the ship after a sortie was the really intense time. The landing ship officer signaled to the pilot when the plane was aligned properly for landing. There were five arresting wires across the deck of the ship. The "tail hook" was lowered to catch the plane, and to say it was not dangerous was turning a blind eye to the possible problems. The worst of those problems was "hook skip,"meaning that the plane's hook missed the arresting wires, and a "bolter" was called. The captain then had to apply full power to take off from the short deck, flying off ahead of the ship, to circle around and try another landing. Low fuel was often a condition that added to the problem, making all aboard very tense until the aircraft was safely recovered. One must keep in mind that the ocean was hardly ever "bath tub calm," so all flight deck operations were risky, or exciting, depending on your point of view.

The *Bennington* and Dave made three Western Pacific cruises, each averaging six months in length. They sailed to Japan, Bangkok, Hong Kong, and the Philippines. Dave had the opportunity to fly his S2 to Australia and was amazed to see so many Aussies wearing flip-flops on the flight deck of the carrier *Melbourne*. Very few of the crew had all of their toes.

The ship stayed on Yankee Station in the South China Sea. The activities of the squadron were mainly to fly over Vietnam, find likely targets, then direct the gunfire of the battleship lying off the coast. More than once, the slower planes came back to the carrier with bullet holes in their tail section.

So, what was I doing all of this time? Each time Dave would leave on a cruise with his squadron, I would pack up our apartment, put everything into storage, and return to Modesto to stay with my parents. I knew that is what Dave wanted because then he did not have to worry about me. I spent some time as a substitute teacher, and that helped me pass the time. Before the ship would return, I would go back to Coronado, find us an apartment (rent was $150 per month or less), unpack our things, and have the apartment ready for a happy homecoming.

Between the second and third cruises, Dave was on shore for more than a year. I cannot count how many of the wives became pregnant during that time. We looked like a Planned Parenthood meeting when we played bridge. Our son, David Brian Orozco, was born in the Coronado Hospital on July 6, 1966.

When our son was six months old, Dave's ship deployed again. I went back to Modesto, and my parents were delighted with their first grandchild. He had lovely hair, and I was determined to let it grow until Daddy came home. His hair eventually grew down to his shoulders. When I got rather discourteous remarks about that boy's hair, I looked the person right in the eye and said, "He will get his hair cut when his father gets home from Vietnam." There was no further discussion.

Continental Airlines Pilot David Orozco with his two grandsons, circa 2000.

Modesto being so far from the coast, the feelings of closeness to the war was limited. I did hear from a friend, "Oh, you really do have a husband. I thought you made him up!" Those feelings changed as the fighting escalated to the terrible combat that we all came to see on television.

I am still very proud of my husband's service for his country. He was honorably discharged as a lieutenant, April 1967. His decorations included Navy Air Medal with three Bronze Stars, Meritorious Unit Citation with Bronze Star, National Defense Service Medal, Vietnam Service Medal with three Bronze Stars, and the RVN Gallantry Cross Unit Citation Ribbon.

Dave's flying experience in the Navy enabled him to fly for Continental Airlines, accruing 27,000 hours in B-727, B-707, DC-10, MD-80, and B777 aircraft. He retired from Continental on December 12, 2001, with thirty-five years of excellent service to the company and the traveling public.

Before retiring, Captain Orozco had one last experience when he flew one of the first 777's into Paris. This was right after the horror of the Twin Towers and the Pentagon on September 11, 2001. He checked into the hotel with his entire crew made up of eighteen pilots and flight attendants. As they crossed the lobby, they were accosted by a group of loud, rude, laughing Middle Easterners who were videotaping the Americans while shouting, "We got you good this time!" It was all Dave could do to control his crew, getting them out of the lobby before there was an international incident. I am certain he used leadership skills learned in the Navy and at Continental Air Lines.

Unable to conquer a malignant brain tumor, Dave left me, our son, David, wife Laura, and two grandsons, Andrew and Adam; and our daughter, Susan, on February 4, 2005. He was very much loved and is still missed by all of his family.

146

A UNITED STATES NAVY NURSE

By Jane Stineman Paskowitz
Sacramento Chapter, NSDAR
Sacramento, California

I served as a Navy nurse during the Vietnam War. I was on active duty from my graduation from the University of California Nursing School in San Francisco, June 1967, until December 1969. I served at the United States Naval Hospital, Charleston, South Carolina, the entire time I was in the service. I had applied for a hospital ship as my next assignment but withdrew the request when I married. My husband was a Navy physician, also stationed at Charleston.

Jane Stineman Paskowitz, RN
United States Navy.

There were many reasons I served in the military, the most important one being that they paid for my last year of nursing school. I was obligated to give the Navy two years of service for each year of education they paid.

When I started working, I served as a staff nurse. After some experience, I served as a charge nurse. I was a registered nurse with a Bachelor of Science degree in nursing. My duties were the typical responsibilities of a charge nurse, being responsible for all the activities that occur on a unit. I worked mostly in the Intensive Care Unit but had to rotate occasionally.

Sometimes I'd work in the emergency room, or surgery, or post-surgical units, medical units, infectious disease, or psychiatric wards. One of the most important things nurses did was to train the corpsmen how to function as nurses on the battlefield. We taught them everything from basic first aid and bandaging to starting IV's, giving medications, CPR, all the skills they were likely to need in hostile areas.

I liked military life, especially the nursing. Our hospital had two neurosurgeons. We received the neurosurgical evacuations from Vietnam whose families were in the southeastern part of the United States. The military recognized early on that being close to family helps with healing. It was an exciting time. I learned something new every day.

In the military, order is the rule of the day. There are certain chains of command, ways of doing things. These basic rules of order give you a framework that frees you up from the quandaries: "Should I do it this way or that?" "Should I contact this person or that?" If you do it the military way, it saves a lot of time. There were some things about the military I did not like. For instance, the mandatory receptions and parties. However, I can see that they were necessary to build *esprit de corps*.

The Navy certainly had an impact on my life. The military firmed up my belief in responsibility for actions and the resultant consequences. It made me proud to be an American, and proud that I did my part to serve my country. I know firsthand the hardships and sacrifices Americans have made. The casualties of conflict were not just deaths, they were the ultimate sacrifices for our nation. Throughout their lives, every military member carries experiences of that time. I remember the changes in the corpsmen coming back from Vietnam. You could see in their faces that they had seen unimaginable things and done things they might never talk about. Several of my corpsmen never made it back. I think of how young they were and how willing they were to put their lives on the line to help others. What great young men they were.

I think of all the other casualties of war, not only the dead, but the wounded. There were vast numbers of surgical and medical cases, malaria, parasitic infestations, mental problems, and drug addictions. There were an incredible number of amputations. Many could not be put back the way they were. Many still reside in veterans hospitals. These young men are not the same as when they went to war. Being in the military is a very serious thing. I'm glad I was able to give service to my country. It was an honor and a privilege.

MY FLYING TIGER DAYS

By Leslie Laird Pfeifer
Anne Loucks Chapter, NSDAR
Martinez, California

As a flight attendant for Flying Tiger Airlines in the 1960's, I worked on military charters to Vietnam. We transported military personnel from Air Force bases in the United States (Travis, McChord, El Toro) to Air Force bases in Vietnam (Da Nang, Bien Hoa, Cam Ranh Bay, and Tan Son Nhut). Each trip was a week long with layovers in Anchorage, then on to either Okinawa, Japan, or bases in the Philippines: Kadena, Yokota, or Clark. The last leg of each trip was to Vietnam and back with minimal time on the ground. Then, another layover in Okinawa, Japan, or the Philippines. After our layover, we picked up a flight and flew back home to an American air base. This was an eighteen-hour nonstop flight. I made approximately seventy-five trips into Vietnam between 1967 and 1970.

Flying Tiger's fleet of DC Stretch 8's held 365 military passengers each. The configuration was a center aisle with three seats on either side. There were no divided cabins. From front to back, the cabin looked like three long buses of service men. The majority of the passengers were young Army recruits headed for their duty stations in Vietnam. Eight flight attendants took care of them during those long flights.

Flying into Vietnam was dangerous. After the Tet Offensive in 1968, we were ordered to land only during the day and to stay a minimal time on the ground. However, many times we landed at night with the cabin lights off. The Da Nang landing strip was adjacent to a Marine patrolled area, and we would see flares. If the airstrip was ever under direct attack, we had instructions: deplane, run across the tarmac, and jump into an assigned foxhole on top of a Marine and his machine gun. We were told to zigzag, not to run straight. We all joked about this. We decided we would go down with the plane rather than get shot by a Marine startled by eight women jumping on top of him. There were bullet holes in the belly of the aircraft. Were we scared? No. We had no fear. We were doing our jobs.

I was young, full of excitement andI loved the adventure of my job. However, my first flight brought a stark thunderbolt of reality. A young soldier engaged me in conversation throughout the flight. He was probably eighteen years old, drafted into the Army, and was most likely going to Vietnam and the frontlines. Toward the end of the flight, he said he wanted me to have something. He gave me his rosary beads. I said I could not accept them. He insisted I take them. We wrote a few times, then I stopped hearing from him. I have kept his rosary beads to this day and have never forgotten him.

On our flights we did everything we could to take care of the troops and make them comfortable on their long journeys to and from Vietnam. Making the Marines smile was nearly impossible, but we tried. We were supposed to collect all weapons and put them in the cockpit, but the Marines kept theirs with them at all times.

Taking troops over to Vietnam and returning with those who had completed their thirteen-month tour of duty were completely different experiences. The mood going over was one of somber fear. Upon landing in Vietnam, the aircraft door opened to 110-degree heat and 85 percent humidity. We stationed ourselves at the top and bottom of the stairs and bid goodbye to each soldier.

We would take on Marines in Da Nang straight out of the jungle for their homeward flight. They were hot, dirty, exhausted, almost dazed. We welcomed 365 sweaty soldiers onto our semi-air conditioned aircraft. Some had a look of desperation. As we took off and got airborne, they would loosen up, but showed no sense of relaxation until we were well out of Asian airspace. They were so grateful for cold milk, and were happy to see American girls. They could not do enough for us. If we were struggling with a heavy metal bin in the galley, they would be in there to help. The meals we served were government issue, but there were no complaints. The soldiers would do a lot of sleeping. During the long hours, we did a lot of laughing and talking, too. The soldiers and officers would give us their patches and medals. We collected many and wore them on our in-flight uniforms. Once we got close to home and stateside, there was jubilation. Soldiers kissed the ground when they deplaned.

I developed a deep respect for all those who served in Vietnam. They came home to an ungrateful nation. I lived in Berkeley during those years and witnessed protest marches and anti-war demonstrations. I did not, could not, participate. I had just returned from being with planeloads of men serving their country. Many were seriously wounded physically and mentally. Our boys were dying, and our nation seemed largely oblivious.

Flight Attendant Leslie Laird and Flying Tiger Airlines' flight crew.

If it were not for the Vietnam War, I would not have met the man who became my husband. My career ended because flight attendants were not allowed to be married in those days. Dave was in the Navy and made it a career. We were married in the chapel on Treasure Island in 1972.

A reunion of twenty-five Flying Tiger flight attendants who flew the military charters in the 1960's was recently held at the California Vietnam Veterans Memorial on the Capitol grounds in Sacramento. It was a bittersweet, tearful, happy reunion. We held each other as we read on the memorial's walls the names of 5,000 Californians killed in Vietnam. We sang the national anthem and left American flags and roses. Those of us who transported military personnel during the Vietnam War share a strong bond. The experience profoundly affected all of our lives.

THE LIFE AND LEGACY OF DANIEL CHENEY

By Donna Cheney Pinckney
Santa Margarita Chapter, NSDAR
Oceanside, California

First Lieutenant Daniel Bernard Cheney, recipient of the Distinguished Flying Cross, was born January 28, 1947. He served in Vietnam, December 20, 1968 - January 6, 1969. On that day in 1969, he was piloting a 17th Cavalry Cobra helicopter when a nearby helicopter was shot down. In a valiant action to save the lives of its pilot and observer, Dan engaged the enemy, providing cover for the crew's rescue. He was killed instantly when his helicopter crashed in a barrage of enemy fire.

Captain Daniel Bernard Cheney
United States Army

I was twelve years older than my cousin Dan. He came into my life when he was eight months old. His father was a Marine who fought in the South Pacific during WWII. He relocated his family to find a new beginning after the war. In the process, the family lived with us for a few months. I instantly adopted Dan as the baby brother I had always wanted. I happily welcomed his two sisters, glad to have cousins nearby. We spent a lot of time together until my family moved to California. Then we saw each other only sporadically. However, we always kept in touch, and I was thrilled to learn about his interests and activities. When Dan was six years old, my dad brought him on his first airplane ride to spend an unforgettable summer with me in California.

Then, we all grew up. I went away to college, married, and started a family. My sister and Dan's two sisters did the same. Dan had a wonderful childhood growing up in a loving family. His life was highlighted by many successes, including his Little League baseball team winning a National Championship. He attended college and graduated with honors from the Army Officer Candidate School. He earned his wings at the Army Flight School in Alabama.

Dan was in Vietnam for a brief time when, just three weeks before his twenty-second birthday, he was killed. Our entire family was devastated by the news. Just before leaving, Dan became engaged. The engagement announcement was printed in the local paper on the day he died. Two days later, the paper published the article about the death of a local helicopter pilot who died in Vienam. We didn't even have time to get used to the idea that he was there.

Dan's funeral in Vancouver, Washington, was attended by a multitude of grieving family members, including me. The church was packed with friends, classmates, and others showing support for the family. There was no consoling Dan's parents. His father sought refuge in alcohol, an issue he resolved before his death. His mother's heart was irreparably broken. However, that was not to be the end of Dan's story.

Dan's legacy - PeaceTrees Vietnam

As the months passed, God planted a seed in the heart of Dan's youngest sister, Jerilyn Cheney Brusseau. With a family of three children, she started a business, baking and selling cookies from her kitchen. Soon she renovated an old garage, turning it into a bakery. The bakery became a popular bakery/cafe. Jerilyn turned to food consulting. In 1985, she was hired by a company to create the perfect cinnamon roll, known today as Cinnabon. In the family, Jerilyn is known as the "Cinnabon Lady."

In her spare time, Jerilyn started a non-governmental organzation called Peace Table. Along the way, she met and married Danaan Parry, a physicist who turned from designing weapons to becomingan internationally known author, lecturer, and facilitator in conflict resolution. They combined their peacemaking efforts.

In 1995, it was announced that the United States and Vietnam had established diplomatic relations. Jerilyn and Danaan flew to Washington, D.C. where they met with Vietnamese Embassy staff members. They requested support for an effort to bring the people of America and Vietnam close together in a constructive relationship of friendship and peace. Thus, PeaceTrees Vietnam was born.

On their first visit to Vietnam, Jerilyn and Danaan learned that Quang Tri Province in central Vietnam had seen the heaviest fighting of the war. Today, the land remains 83 percent polluted with unexploded ordnance (UXO). Since the war ended, there have been more than 8,000 victims of these weapons in Quang Tri Province, with injuries and fatalities still occurring, mostly among children and farmers.

By November 1996, PeaceTrees Vietnam had raised $220,000, and an eighteen-acre battlefield had been cleared of explosives. As Jerilyn and Danaan prepared to leave Seattle with forty-three volunteers and veterans, Danaan suffered a massive heart attack and died. The day after his memorial service, Jerilyn and her volunteers traveled to Vietnam. They were soon followed by others, who made the trip to plant indigenous trees on the cleared land and to provide food and clothing to the poor. Most importantly, they went to build friendship and understanding so that the sad chapters of the Vietnam War will not be repeated.

These delegations continue today: de-mining, clearing and planting the land. To date, more than 84,000 UXO have been removed and destroyed, more than 600 acres have been cleared, over 43,500 trees have been planted, and mine risk and accident prevention education has been provided for almost 87,000 Vietnamese. Assistance to 952 UXO victims with medical treatment, educational scholarships and micro-credit grants has also been given. PeaceTrees Vietnam has also built many kindergartens in Quang Tri Province. On some of the first cleared land, a Land Mine Education Center was erected. In 2002, PeaceTrees Vietnam completed a Friendship Village of 100 homes near Dong Ha for land mine victims and their families.

At age ninety-four, Dan's mother, my aunt Rae, decided she could help the effort by sending thank you notes to donors. To date, she has written more than 7,500 letters. Now she is involved in every aspect of the organization. She has experienced a profound transformation from anger and pain to healing and service. She loves to associate with veterans and to hear their stories. She is often asked to speak at annual meetings of the Vietnam Helicopter Pilots Association.

Years ago, I told Aunt Rae that when she was ready to go to Vietnam, I would go with her. That opportunity came in 2010 as Peace-Trees Vietnam celebrated fifteen years of service with the dedication of the Dan Cheney Kindergarten and The Mothers' Peace Library, dedicated to Rae and all American and Vietnamese mothers who lost sons and daughters during the war. As Ambassador LeVan Bang noted, "It is the peace between the mothers that is the most important peace of all."

The ache in my heart does not go away. To this day, Dan remains in my heart as the beloved brother I never had. He would be celebrating his sixty-seventh birthday as I write this. We cannot help but wonder what his life would have been and who he would have become. We do know his life would have been full of courage, humor, success, love, and, always, an abiding love of his country for which he gave his life. It is comforting to know that Dan's legacy of service lives on through PeaceTrees Vietnam.*

Left to right, 2007: Donna Cheney Pinckney, Jerilyn Cheney Parry Brusseau, Rae Cheney.

*PeaceTrees Vietnam: *www.peacetreesvietnam.org*

ON THE ROAD, AGAIN!

By Glynice Pomykal
Josefa Higuera Livermore Chapter, NSDAR
Livermore, California

My life as a Navy wife began in 1965 when Lieutenant JG Glenn Pomykal and I were married in Mill Valley, California. At the time, Glenn was a general line officer, which meant his time was spent at sea. We met in Long Beach, California where I was teaching and he was a young Naval officer first serving on the USS *Leader* (MSO 490), and then on the USS *Topeka* (GLG-8).

Glenn's first tour of duty after we were married was at the U.S. Naval Postgraduate School in Monterey, California, where he studied in the Nuclear Engineering Effects Program. During this time I taught at the Joseph P. Stillwell School on the Fort Ord Army Base where many of my students' fathers were either deploying to Vietnam or just returning from a tour there. It was during our stay in Monterey that our first daughter, Susan, was born. She was only nine months old when we left Monterey two years later.

Our next move was back to Long Beach, California where Glenn immediately flew out to the Western Pacific to join the USS *Illusive* (MSO 448) for a six-month deployment. He returned about six weeks before our second daughter, Carey, was born. When Carey was only four months old, Glenn returned for another tour of duty at sea, leaving me with two very young children. It was because of very dear civilian friends - Marilyn, Bob, Dorothy, Harold and Esther - that I was able to keep my sanity. They helped me in so many ways, and I will never be able to thank them enough for all they did for me. Also during this time, we lost my only cousin on my mother's side, Michael Doane, a proud nineteen-year-old Marine who died in Vietnam.

Just before Carey's first birthday, Glenn's ship returned to port. As a baby, Carey was very attached to me and didn't like staying with others. However, I left Carey at home with a friend and went to meet the ship with many of the other families. It is a very memorable experience for families and friends to meet a ship returning from a long deployment. When we returned home with Glenn, Carey amazingly went to him with no fuss. Since she and her sister, Susan, told their daddy's picture, "Goodnight," every night, she already knew who he was.

Following Glenn's return, he was next assigned to go to the Destroyer School in Newport, Rhode Island. We drove across country with a nearly three-year-old and a one-year-old. This was a six-month tour of duty, so we all enjoyed our precious time together and did as much together as we could while we were there. Susan had her third birthday while we were in Newport, the first time Glenn had been home to celebrate one of her birthdays.

Six months later we were once again headed back across the country to Long Beach where Glenn flew out to the USS *Collette* (DD-730) for another tour of sea duty. We arrived in California in time to spend Christmas with our friends. This was the first Christmas Glenn had with Susan since she was three months old. Carey was now 18 months old, and I was expecting our third child in February. While the Navy allowed Glenn time to get us settled, he was not allowed to stay home until our son, Andrew, was born. Glenn left one month before Andy arrived. It was our friend, Harold, who took me to the hospital in the middle of the night, and he stayed with me until Andy was born. Again, as they had for all the time we lived in the Long Beach area, our friends stepped in and took care of the kids when I was too sick to take care of them, or just to give me a much-needed break.

Glenn's ship returned back to Long Beach when Andy was one month old. During this stay in port, the *Collette* was in and out on training maneuvers. The USS *Collette* was expected to return to the Western Pacific for another tour of duty when the ship was decommissioned. December 1970, Glenn's next assignment was at the Livermore National Laboratory as a military research associate. We were thrilled that he would have a two-year tour of duty with Glenn being home every night. We arrived shortly before Christmas.

Susan was now four by this time, Carey two and a half, and Andy was ten months old. We had our first Christmas as a family in our own home. At the end of two years in Livermore, Glenn resigned his commission as a lieutenant commander, and we moved to Los Alamos, New Mexico. We returned to Livermore two years later.

In many ways this was a difficult and lonely life, but it was well worth it in many ways. It gave us the opportunity to live in some of the most unusual and beautiful places in the United States. We made so many wonderful friends along the way, some who have been part of our family ever since.

IN COLLEGE AND MARRIED TO A MARINE

By Jan Quigley
Rancho Buena Vista Chapter, NSDAR
Vista, California

I entered the University of California Los Angeles, September 1969, just as many of my male classmates were leaving for the Vietnam War. I have often wondered how many did not return home to their families.

In 1970 and 1971, the memories of my college years at UCLA were dimmed by violent protests and the bombing of the Navy Wardroom in the Men's Gymnasium Building. During campus protests, the lovely carved wooden doors of the gym were splintered by battering rams. I stood at the top of Janss Steps with tears streaming down my face as demonstrators broke the doors to the building that was home to the Naval Reserve Officer Training Corps and the Anchors (the women's auxiliary to the NROTC on campus).

UCLA's NROTC and Anchors' drill teams had just brought back seven trophies from the annual Governor of Arizona's drill meet. After the bombing of the Naval ROTC Wardroom, they were in a melted heap of broken glass. The bomb was smuggled

April, 1972: Jan Quigley; her husband, Lieutenant Ken Quigley (United States Marine Corps); and their son, Mark Quigley.

in a briefcase and slipped under a sofa in the wardroom when no one was watching. Its timer had been set for 2:00 a.m. Luckily, the janitor was not there when it exploded. What a close call. We played bridge and congregated in that very room between classes.

The midshipmen were told not to wear their uniforms on campus during the campus violence. I could not sleep all night as the helicopters patrolled, circling my sorority house on the southeast side of campus.

In spring 1974, my husband, a lieutenant in the United States Marine Corps, left for Okinawa, Japan. It was near the end of the Vietnam War, and soon after arriving in Okinawa, he deployed on a ship. We exchanged letters. I wrote every single day. When I received his letters, I would put them in order of date written. We had tape recorders and sent tapes back and forth. Our son, Mark, was three years old when his father deployed. He would get excited upon hearing Daddy's voice on the recorder. Who cared if the news was a month old?

Often times I would ask Ken where his ship was headed, and he would say, "I can't tell you." I would sometimes get a call from a ham radio operator who would patch a phone call through from my husband. It's difficult to have a conversation with two radio operators listening in. During Ken's deployment, I worked as a Navy Relief Society Volunteer at Camp Pendleton to help pass the time while our son attended preschool on the base.

I heard the stories about the tent city that was constructed at Camp Pendleton for the Vietnamese refugees. My girlfriend's husband was a supply officer for the base, and she told me he was trying to acquire 6,000 pair of chopsticks. The adult refugees could manage a spoon, but the children could not. They needed their chopsticks. Her husband said that the toilet tissue kept disappearing from the portable facilities in the tent city. They finally figured out that the Vietnamese women were hoarding it in their suitcases. They had given up all their belongings for freedom and now were hoarding toilet tissue. We felt so sorry for the refugees, but we often heard about families or churches that were sponsoring them. Those refugees were soon on their way via bus to another city or state to start new lives in the United States.

While he was at Subic Bay in the Philippines, my husband's job was to board the boats before the refugees could disembark, and confiscate anything that could be considered a weapon. The most startling story I heard my husband tell occurred during the evacuation of Saigon. The South Vietnamese pilots flew helicopters out of Saigon and landed on United States Navy ships. The helicopters had to be pushed off the ships to their graves on the ocean bottom. Such a waste of money. However, there was not room to bring all the aircraft back to bases in the United States.

When Ken was deployed many years later during Desert Storm, he had a phone and would call me weekly. Then, during the Iraq War, I would tell the new Marine wives how lucky they were to have e-mail and to hear from their husbands daily. Amazing how social media has changed things.

I am envious of today's college students who do not have to experience the distractions we had during the Vietnam War: constant protests, university shootings, bombings, and other destructive behavior. The late 1960's and early 1970's were trying to say the least.

BRACELETS IN TIME

By Amanda Young Rigby
Rancho Buena Vista Chapter, NSDAR
Vista, California

As a child of the 1960's and 1970's, the Vietnam War should have been something that played out in the background as I sat on the merry-go-round and made daisy chains for my hair. But that was not to be.

Yes, we watched on the nightly news as the atrocities of war unfolded right there in our living room. More than that, my dad, Phil Poisson, was in the United States Navy, attached to a search-and-rescue squadron. He was the one dangling from a helicopter, tethered to the end of a cable. Reaching into the jungles of Vietnam, he was trying his damnedest to pull a downed pilot to safety before the enemy snatched him away. He and his crew did not always make it in time, and this sad fact ate at Dad's heart and soul.

ATN3 Phil Poisson (on the right) with a pilot he rescued from the Gulf of Tonkin. Date unknown. Poisson went on to receive a battlefield commission and retired from the Navy as an officer.

At one point, MIA/POW bracelets were made and offered for fellow servicemen to wear, to keep vigil and to remember those taken. Over supper one evening, Dad asked us if we children, too, would wear one? Of course, we said we would. After all, we were all in the Navy.

In 1971, our shiny, stainless steel bracelets arrived. All five were the same. They were engraved with "Cmdr. John D. Burns, U.S.N., North Vietnam, October 4, 1966." We wore those bracelets every day until March 1973, when it was confirmed that Commander Burns was among the 591 POW's who came home as part of Operation Homecoming. Many other POW's would come later, and some not at all, but ours was home. Finally home.

Instead of simply taking our bracelets off and tucking them away, Mom and Dad wanted to send them to Commander Burns. They wanted him to know that he hadn't been forgotten and that we were glad he was home. Mom contacted the liaison working with the returnees at Balboa Naval Hospital here in San Diego where we live. He was surprised to learn that not only had an entire family worn bracelets, but that we all had worn the same name. He asked if we would come to the hospital and give the bracelets to Commander Burns personally. We were honored.

Once we arrived at the hospital, I remember feeling such sadness. Overhearing stories from Dad (that Mom tried to edit) or from our friends' dads and watching the news, my thirteen-year-old self understood only a fraction of what these men had endured. However, it was enough to scare me, and it made me sad. Some of the men I saw there looked lost. Their eyes seemed so vacant. I vividly remember the starkness. Others seemed to search the faces of passersby for answers, comfort, understanding, or even judgment. I am sure all my face showed was how sad I was for them. I remember the quiet and the solemnity of the hospital. It was just so quiet. They were so quiet.

A photographer had been sent to join us that day. Apparently, it was quite a thing we had done, a whole family wearing these bracelets.

When we entered the room, Commander Burns was seated in a chair, dressed in his full uniform. He looked sharp and crisp. I had not expected that. We sat and visited for a few minutes. We told him how glad we were to have him home again. We told him we had prayed for his safe return. We exchanged pleasantries. What do you say to someone who has not only had seven years taken from his life, but experienced torture as well?

With Commander Burns at the Balboa Naval Hospital, San Diego. Left to right: Amanda's brother, Ed Young; brother, Lyn Young; her father, Phil Poisson; Commander John D. Burns; her mother, Serena Poisson; and Amanda Young Rigby.

After we visited a bit, the photographer wanted to get the photo of us giving commander Burns our bracelets. Mom and Dad were seated next to the Commander while the children were told to kneel down in front of him. As we knelt, Commander Burns looked down at us and became emotional. I don't remember this, but Mom recalls him saying that he was so moved to have children there. He knew the sailors supported them and figured the spouses probably did as well, but to have the children think about him everyday was quite unexpected and overwhelming. We did not want to intrude on his emotions, so we left the room. If they had let me, I would have hugged him, tightly. He needed a hug.

When we went back into his room, it was decided that we should not kneel. This is the photo you see above. The book on his lap was a gift from Mom. It is a book on friendship, and it was her hope that even in a small way, it might bring comfort to him. The expression on his face is a mix of so many emotions: disbelief, gratitude, love, and others I could not comprehend at the time. His emotion was real, and it was raw. He was grateful not to have been forgotten, and to be home. In my young mind, he was home safe. When I look at this photo, and I see myself watching him, I think back to his raw emotions, his gratitude, and his sadness. I still cry.

I never stop thinking about Commander John D. Burns, or his family. I have often thought how he might be doing on any given day, including my wedding day. I do know that he remained in the Navy, retiring as a captain. He has also served as an officer for a POW service organization. I still wish him well....and wish I had given him that hug.

My Vietnam experience did not end that day with Commander Burns. Dad continued his service, jumping out of perfectly good helicopters, trying valiantly to rescue every pilot he could. As we worried about him every day, he worried for those he could not reach. Dad was a true hero, and because of him, many, many others are alive today. While in Vietnam, he was exposed to Agent Orange and suffered medical issues later in life, including leukemia, from which he died in 2011. Here in San Diego, his funeral was standing room only. Six other services were held for him around the globe.

My husband is also a Vietnam veteran, having served in the Army. He, too, has suffered medical issues as a result of his exposure to Agent Orange. In March 2011, while driving home from the CSS-DAR Conference in Irvine where our daughter had debuted, he suffered a massive stroke. Vietnam continues to play out everyday in my life. I am no longer just a wife, but a caregiver and advocate as well.

In 1985, I saw a woman wearing a POW bracelet, and I asked about it. It was then that I came to realize that not everyone came home from Vietnam. I knew I wanted another bracelet. I received the bracelet for LCDR James Kelly Patterson, shot down over North Vietnam on May 19, 1967. There have been reports of him being alive, still held captive. A news program did a story about him a couple of years back. I have been wearing his bracelet for thirty years, and I wait for his return.

SOLE SURVIVING SONS

By Bonnie Muir Shanks
Western Shores Chapter, NSDAR
Long Beach, California

Since the Civil War, the United States government has made attempts not to send armed service personnel into a war zone who were the last of a family line. Abraham Lincoln knew this too well when writing a letter to a woman who lost all five of her sons to that war. My brother and my husband were both examples of the application of this policy during the Vietnam era. Both served in the Marine Corps during that time. My husband joined the Marines voluntarily, and my brother was drafted into the Marine Corps.

Years after the conflict, my brother, Frederic Woodson Muir, and I talked of his experience in the Corps. He wondered how it was that he was spared from going to Vietnam.

While my brother was in boot camp, I was living with my father in Millington, Tennessee. My father settled there after retiring from a career in the Navy. He spent many nights typing letters. One evening, I finally got curious and asked him who he was writing to. He replied that he was doing all he could to keep his one and only son out of this war. He also said he didn't spend over twenty years serving in the Navy not to have some kind of pull to accomplish this. These letters must have worked because my brother was never sent to Vietnam.

My brother told me that while he was in the Corps, he had orders three different times to go to Vietnam. However, within hours of being transferred overseas, his orders were cancelled. On one occasion, my brother said he reported to the base commander. While he was standing at attention in front of this high-ranking officer, the commander replied, "I just wanted to see what you look like. Dismissed!"

Although my husband, Bruce Howard Shanks, Jr., was an enlisted man, he had a similar experience. He also reported to a high-ranking officer and was asked if he wanted to exercise the option of staying out of the Vietnam War zone. My husband said, "No." However, later on when he was in the jungle, dealing with persistent rain and continual leech removal, he wondered why he didn't exercise that option. My husband received a "million dollar wound" while fighting in the jungle and was medevaced home.

Knowing my husband, I doubt whether he would have changed his mind about going to Vietnam. As it turned out, he was blessed to come home injured, receive a Purple Heart, and be promoted to sergeant. He continued to serve in the Marine Corps as an instructor, and never returned to Vietnam.

THE WAY WE WERE

By Jennifer Smith
Linares Chapter, NSDAR
San Diego, California

Merriam-Webster's online dictionary defines "commemorate" as, "To exist or be done in order to remind people of an important event or person from the past." As we commemorate the fiftieth anniversary of the Vietnam War, we stir up bittersweet memories of people and events; and our memories bring on a mixed bag of emotions.

I graduated from college in 1969. Like many young Southern women of the time, I married shortly after finishing school. Most of us "Southern ladies" weren't politically oriented one way or the other, but we did sense that there was more to the world than what we saw in our community.

Marrying a handsome, young Air Force pilot-seemed like the perfect avenue to adventure, especially when one is in love; and we certainly

Mr. and Mrs. Stephen Bryce Johnston leave on their honeymoon, June 1969.

did have adventures. Our first Air Force home was in Sacramento - a new city for us in a new state. However, the Air Force doesn't keep people in one spot for too long. Within six months, Steve had orders to Otis Air Force Base on Cape Cod, Massachusetts. Oh my, what a change of pace Cape Cod was for a pair of Southerners, especially learning to translate those strange Boston accents to "real" English...at least the way we spoke it.

Life was good at Otis. However, that tour only lasted a year before new orders arrived, sending us to George Air Force Base in Victorville, California. That is where Steve was to go through F-4 Phantom training. Sacramento had been great, but we quickly learned that Victorville was in a different part of the state...a little more arid with far fewer people.

When you lived on an Air Force base, you tended to become isolated from what transpired around you. We always knew there were issues swirling around our nation that hadn't touched us as they had many families throughout the country. However, it wasn't until we arrived at George Air Force Base that it really sank in. Steve was being trained to fly in fighters over North Vietnam. When he left for a year at Udorn Air Base in Thailand - flying night missions over Hanoi - I remained at George Air Force Base. I worked as a Red Cross volunteer, co-leading a group of Girl Scouts, and playing many games of bridge with the other officers' wives. But then, suddenly, reality and the Vietnam War touched me in a tangible way. Steve's plane went down on January 4, 1973. He and the other crewmember ejected, but he didn't survive. He was the last Oklahoman to die in the Vietnam War. Life had definitely changed.

Captain Stephen Bryce Johnston,
United States Air Force,
March 3, 1972.

More than forty years have passed since I had my chilling home visit at George Air Force Base from the wing commander, the chaplain, the squadron flight surgeon, other support, personnel and sympathetic wives. Yes, even though we all knew that flying was especially dangerous in a war zone, it was a shock knowing that my husband was gone. No one else we knew had died in Vietnam, but life is strange that way. Within two weeks, I was making my way as a twenty-five-year-old widow in Austin, Texas, and part of the Veterans Administration system. "The way we were" had taken a drastic turn. It wasn't the adventure I had been looking for three years earlier, but life does go on for those who are left behind.

Through the years, I found the love of my life. He was, ironically, another Air Force pilot. I have survived the Iranian Revolution, served as a White House volunteer, adopted a beautiful Costa Rican infant thirty-two years ago, and I've traveled the world.

Bitter and sweet, the Vietnam War certainly changed my life and the lives of countless others. Through my experiences, I've learned to appreciate each day with all its blessings, to always value and hold close my loved ones, and to look outside myself for opportunities to help the less fortunate, especially those in the Armed Forces. But life's adventures do continue, and I am thankful that the commemoration of the Vietnam War prompts reflections about the way we were, as well as the way we are today.

Life is good that way. May we never forget.

A CHILD'S REMEMBRANCES

By Connie Soloway
Conejo Valley Chapter, NSDAR
Thousand Oaks, California

I was just a young child during the time of the Vietnam War, but I do have several distinct memories that relate to the war. I remember our bulletin board project in my third-grade classroom at Meadowlane Elementary School, in Hialeah, Florida. Our teacher, Mrs. Michaelson, impressed upon us the importance of always being up-to-date on current events. One of the bulletin boards in our classroom was dedicated to current events. One quadrant of that bulletin board was devoted to the Vietnam War.

Even though we were only in third grade, Mrs. Michaelson encouraged us to read the newspaper. She gave us extra credit if we brought articles to share with the class. I remember that few kids in my class brought in articles for the Vietnam War quadrant. Because I liked being allowed to pin an article up on that bulletin board, bringing in articles about the Vietnam War became my project.

I brought in an article about the tunnels used by Cambodian guerilla fighters. I wondered why the Cambodians were fighting in a neighboring country. When I read that Pol Pot forced his countrymen to leave their city homes to labor on collective farms, I learned that leaders are not always beneficent. Another article about military aircraft mechanics taught me that not everybody in the military marched through jungles carrying guns.

The article that made the biggest impact introduced me to Agent Orange. I remember being horrified by the thought of airplanes spraying a chemical on the trees that caused them to die. In my child's mind, I pictured this as being an instantaneous thing and was very sad about it. For me, this was something I could relate to because, living in South Florida, we had airplanes spraying a pesticide mist almost daily to control mosquitos. I was afraid that they would spray Agent Orange over our neighborhood by mistake.

I distinctly remember the daily war updates during the evening news.

The most famous news broadcasters of the time were Walter Cronkite on CBS, and the team of Chet Huntley and David Brinkley on NBC. Every night, they updated the death toll. I also remember stories about the Paris peace talks and wondering why those people in France were taking so long. I thought that ending a war was as simple as saying, "I surrender!"

Third, my nextdoor neighbor enlisted without his parents' knowledge or consent. His parents were both angry and distraught. When my neighbor returned he was a changed person, and not in a good way. He was very, very angry. I remember my parents admonishing us to stay away from him and not to allow him into our home. His parents would not even allow him into their house after a while. He lived in their garage for a few months, and then he was gone. I never saw him again.

Finally, Sharyn Sapp was our babysitter. She lived across the street, and we loved her dearly. She went way to college and graduated. She came home from graduate school engaged to a Vietnam war hero. Her fiancé was Captain Hugh L. Mills, Jr., a highly-decorated Scout helicopter pilot. During the Vietnam war, Captain Mills held the distinction of being the most frequelty downed pilot in the United States Army. He was an exceptionally genial young man, and we loved hearing his many war stories. Eventually, he compiled his stories into a book, *Low Level Hell* (Presidio Press, 2000). In 1974, my sister and I were junior bridesmaids in their wonderful military wedding. Shortly afterward, Captain Mills became Colonel Mills. He and Sharyn moved to Germany where he commanded an Army air base. To learn more about Colonel Mills, see: *http://lstribune. neUleessummit-news/community/lieutenant-colonel-hugh-1.-mills-jr.-retired.htm.*

While writing this, I look back upon that time of my life, and I am astounded to realize how a war being fought so far away impacted a young child back home. How must today's wars, where the threat of terrorism here at home is infinitely more real, be impacting today's children?

LONELY IN UPLAND

By Martha "Marty" Sommercamp
De Anza Chapter, NSDAR
Encinitas, California

My introduction to the Vietnam War came as the new bride of an Air Force officer. My husband, Captain John Sommercamp, was assigned to Travis Air Force Base, near Sacramento, California. I knew where Vietnam was, but I was unaware of what was about to occur. My husband was a navigator with the Military Airlift Command that flew C-130 cargo planes. I was from a Navy family, so I knew the drill of being alone.

At first, John flew to exotic places like New Zealand, Australia, India, Europe, Thailand, and Turkey. Then the planes began to fly mostly to Southeast Asia. Soon, John was regularly enroute to Saigon: cargo in, bodies out. At first, the cargo was things like fencing and odd cases of Campbell's asparagus soup. The military was gearing up for hostilities.

I felt quite comfortable that we would remain at Travis Air Force Base. I went to college as John was gone about three-fourths of the time. There was a rule that if

Captain John Sommercamp,
United States Air Force

you were out of the country more that 270 days, you would not be sent to Vietnam. Just as I was starting a new semester, John received orders to Da Nang, Vietnam. So much for the rule! We had to move out of our quarters in five days, and I dropped out of school. He had to go to Eglin Air Force Base in Florida for three months of training, so I tagged along. He was assigned to a rescue squadron of HU-16's, which were old WWII-era seaplanes. They were going to be rescuing downed fighter pilots off North Vietnam.

We decided that I would move home to live with my parents in Upland, California, and I would start back to college after he left for Vietnam. John felt it would best for me to be with my family if something happened to him. I made the trip back to Travis Air Force Base in May 1966 to see John off to Vietnam for a year-long assignment. It was a very sad time, and the farewell at the airport was gut wrenching. I was twenty-two years old.

I returned to college shortly after he left. I was busy with school and my family. The war protests had started in colleges around the country My dad felt that I should not share my situation with anyone at school. So I made few friends. I just went to school and did my work. As professors and students held heated classroom discussions about Vietnam, I just sat and did my work.

My communication with John was difficult. We wrote lots of letters and sent tapes, but these often took two weeks for delivery.

Captain John Sommercamp's flight crew with an HU-16, Da Nang, Vietnam. Captain Sommercamp is third from the left.

Unlike today, there were no cell phones or email, so I only spoke with him the few times he was out of Vietnam. This rare communication was very expensive. A ten-minute call was over $100.

I got my first scare one day when I came home from school. My husband's parents called. People in their small town of Beaumont, California, were telling them they had heard my husband's name on a radio or television broadcast. My dad did not think that anything happened because no one from the Air Force had contacted me. The next morning, my dad woke me up to show me the front page of the *Los Angeles Times*. It was an HU-16 making a water rescue off North Vietnam. My husband was able to call to explain what happened, but I had a nervous twenty-four hours until I heard his voice! John received his first Distinguished Flying Cross for the rescue of two Navy fighter pilots.

At Christmas break, I flew to Hawaii to be with John during his five-day leave. It was just perfect until he had to return on Christmas Day. I returned home and started back to college. He wrote often, sometimes sharing his frustration with the war. I did not worry. I naively thought that they could always rescue themselves if something happened to their plane.

Tragically, one of the squadron planes disappeared while on station off North Vietnam. Fortunately, my husband was not on the plane. He was in Thailand with another plane that was undergoing some repairs. They searched for days and never found so much as a life jacket or a piece of the plane. I got the news in a letter just before I went back to school. It was just heartbreaking. I knew the crew members and some of their families.

Shortly after that loss, I had another big scare. I was sleeping in because I did not have class. I got up and opened the shutters and looked out the window to the street. Parked in front of our house was a blue Air Force staff car with two Air Force officers in it. At the same time, my mom was at the kitchen sink doing the breakfast dishes when she saw the blue car parked in front of my bedroom. She called my dad at work to come home immediately. She gently called to me that I should get dressed quickly. My life passed before me in those moments. Would I be a young widow in a life without John? As it turned out, the car was lost and had accidently stopped right in front of my bedroom window. My dad suggested to them that they should not park in front of random houses. I have always wondered whose house they went to that day.

My husband came home safely in April 1967 just before his year was up. John was awarded two Distinguished Flying Crosses and seven Air Medals. It was a difficult time in our country. John lost friends and West Point classmates. I often look back to that moment when I feared John might be dead, and I realize that God had a different plan for us.

Officers' Club and barracks, Da Nang, Vietnam

View from the cockpit, flying over the Gulf of Tonkin, North Vietnam

MY BROTHER, RAYMOND HERNANDEZ

By Josie Stordahl
John Greenleaf Whittier Chapter, NSDAR
Whittier, California

My brother, Raymond Hernandez, and I were very close as children. He was the oldest. I followed thirteen months later. We were very competitive and inseparable in school and games. I married two months after I turned fifteen, and at twenty-eight with six daughters, I realized my future appeared very bleak. I looked at my brother's Vietnam service, with all the controversies, and saw his continued pride and strength in serving his country. Taking that strength and inspiration, and remembering our competitiveness, I went to work and back to school. I studied electronics and television repair, a field that had no women in my class or in my job. There were many days I felt like giving up, but I compared myself to my brother and continued.

Machinist Mate Chief (MM) Raymond Hernandez, United States Navy

At age seventeen, Raymond joined the United States Navy in San Diego, California, February 24, 1959. He retired, May 9, 1978 as a machinist mate chief. He served on nine different destroyers during that time. Raymond went to Vietnam four times. The last three deployments were aboard the USS *Berkeley*. He served under Commander John F. Frost III and under Commander Jerry A. Dickman.

At that time, the ship was heavily engaged in the Vietnam conflict. During this period the ship participated in numerous linebacker operations, shore bombardment assignments, and as part of surface strike forces into Vinh and Haiphong Harbors during mining operations. Sixteen of Raymond's twenty years in the Navy were spent on destroyers.

In 2010, Raymond rode his Harley-Davidson motorcycle on a "Run for the Wall" ride from California to Washington, D.C. There were an average of 250 Vietnam War veterans riding with him at any given time. The acknowledgement that was not felt before the ride, and that was evident during the event, healed him and filled him with pride for his service to his country. The most poignant story was about an elderly woman standing in a field, waving an American flag and holding a picture of her loved one, who didn't return home from the Vietnam War.

That journey not only honored the riders as Vietnam veterans, but also called attention to the over 58,000 service men and women who didn't survive the Vietnam War. They were all finally recognized as the heroes they are. I am proud of my brother and proud to be a member of the Daughters of the American Revolution.

THE WAR'S INFLUENCE WAS EVERYWHERE

By Ann Lawson Taylor
Sierra Amador Chapter, NSDAR
Jackson, California

My high school and early college years were framed within the context of the Vietnam War. The television at home was always tuned to scenes of violence and bloodshed in the jungle, impassioned protesters screaming as they shook signs of protest, even people lighting themselves on fire in protest. Parents were always scanning the daily paper for enlistment and funeral information, and they were always passionately in favor of, or distressed by, political and other famous figures. Surrounded with constant death, destruction, and passion, I became a bookworm. Chores, Friday nights with *Star Trek*, and Sunday nights with Walt Disney were the exceptions.

Winter, 1973, Turlock, California.
Left to right: Ann Lawson Taylor, her husband,
her younger sister, and two younger brothers.

During the summer of 1969, after my senior year in high school, my friend and I worked on her aunt's ranch. Out on the ranch, mail was anticipated with eagerness and dread. Two of my friend's cousins were in Vietnam, and a third cousin had already been killed. With relief and joy, we would gather to read a letter that arrived from overseas. A single phone call ended the joy; another cousin had been killed. This was a terrible shock to the grieving family. Two of three brothers were now gone. By the time the family gathered for the memorial service, the third and last son of that family had been killed in action. How does one relieve the grief and agony of parents who have lost all three sons? My friend's twin brother was the only young male left to the extended family, and he would be eligible for the draft within a few months.

This hit home deeply. My two closest cousins would also be eligible within months. Everyone I knew at college hovered over the radio throughout the reading of draft lottery numbers. To pick each lottery number, someone would reach into a large jar to pull out an opaque capsule. Tucked inside the capsule was a birth date that would be read aloud and assigned its lottery number, starting with number 001. The person who pulled out the capsule handed it to an official, who opened the capsule, unrolled the paper and announced a date, for example: "September 17...September 17 is lottery number 001." Those with the lowest lottery numbers were drafted unless they were unfit or had a deferment.

Somehow my family escaped, but the war's influence was everywhere. College enrollment postponed draft eligibility. Because of this, all California higher education institutions were filled to overflowing. I met my husband because he registered late at Stanislaus State, the only state college that still had openings. Many students cared little about education and much more about draft avoidance. College was either a place to party before being drafted, or a place to celebrate return from service. During my freshman and sophomore years, even the professors were in the party mode.

The biggest parties at Stanislaus State College, famous throughout the campus and town, were huge and practically ongoing. These were so heavily attended that friendly police would park on the property for hours at a time. The "king" of these parties was a Vietnam veteran named John. One day, John explained that throughout his service in Vietnam, he never expected to return home. He knew he would be killed. A month prior to the end of his service, he realized he might make it out alive. I don't know if it's true, but he said he spent that month in his tent, refusing to come out. Amazingly, he was allowed to stay in that tent. On returning home, his life became one big party. I met John ten years later at a reunion of friends. He had become a professional party organizer. John was paid to party for six months of the year, and he traveled the other six months.

It still amazes me that all of my uncles and great uncles served in WWII, yet not one of my male cousins served during Vietnam. My brothers were too young during the height of the action; and when one got permission for young admission to the Navy, he was not sent to Vietnam.

One lasting effect of the Vietnam War was the change in age for voter eligibility. During the war, the law was changed because if a person was eligible to fight, they should also be eligible to vote. Now, I'm not so sure we made a good decision. In my current perspective, younger voters don't seem to understand the long-range effects of today's vote. The effects of the Vienam War, like other wars, will always be with us.

GARY'S DRAWING

By Deanna Triebold
Sierra Foothills Chapter, NSDAR
Oakhurst, California

I was too young to remember the early years of the Vietnam War. My memories of the war begin in 1967 when my high school boyfriend, Gary David Tice, visited me in the hospital. He announced, "I bet you can't guess what I did on my way to visit you today." Of course, I couldn't guess. I had no idea that he would say. "I joined the Marines!"

Early one summer morning, Gary left for Camp Pendleton and several weeks of boot camp. After he graduated from boot camp, he came home for a couple of weeks' leave to Milpitas, California, while waiting for his duty assignment. He was ordered to the Quang Tri Province at Khe Sanh, Vietnam, in November of 1967.

Gary was a rifleman in the 1st Battalion 9th Marines. This battalion carried the nickname of "The Walking Dead" because of its high casualty rate. This should have been my first clue that Gary was headed into danger, but I was too young and naïve to even think that.

Once Gary arrived and settled in, he began sending me drawings of the views near his station. He was always positive about life and was proud to be a Marine. In the spring of 1968, Gary was promoted to lance corporal.

Several of the girls from Samuel Ayer High School in Milpitas spent hours writing and sending letters to our soldiers in Vietnam. Gary made it a point to request letters for his fellow soldiers if he didn't think they were receiving enough mail from home. It was thoughtful of him to do that, but that was the kind of fellow he was.

Unfortunately, Gary was killed in action on July 17, 1968, by hostile fire. His friend, Lance Corporal T.W. "Rick" Richards, sent a letter to inform me of his death. Gary D. Tice is buried at Golden Gate National Cemetery. Sadly, over time, I lost contact with the soldiers I was writing to. I do often wonder what happened to them and where they are today. I do not know what happened to Gary's Milpitas family.

About six months after Gary's death I met a young sailor who was a radio operator for P3 Orion, stationed at Moffett Field, California. He spent several tours flying over Vietnam, and I'm glad to say, lived through the experience. He has gone with me to the Vietnam Wall to see Gary's name. He, too, was touched by his supreme service to our country.

Here's a picture that Gary drew for me of the area of Khe Sanh where he was assigned.

Lance Corporal Gary David Tice's rendering of his command position, Khe Sanh, Vietnam, April 14, 1968.

ACTING ON A DARE

By Elisabeth Lewis Usborne
Linares Chapter, NSDAR
San Diego, California

In 1963, I was a junior at Denison University in Granville, Ohio. At that time, the draft was in place for males in the United States, and military recruiters visited colleges to recruit college graduate officer candidates. One day, a group of us was playing bridge in the student union. We looked up and saw the Navy recruiters setting up for the day. Someone suggested we all put a dollar on the table and whoever dared to talk to the recruiters would get the pot. I knew nothing about the military, and I took up the challenge. My life was changed forever!

Lieutenant JG Elisabeth Lewis,
a United States Navy WAVE

The recruiters answered my questions and told me about a program for college juniors. I could go to the Officer Candidate School at Newport, Rhode Island, for the summer between my junior and senior year, and either be commissioned as an ensign at graduation or just simply say, "No thank you." I had always been very patriotic but had never envisioned being in the military. However, when I returned to the bridge group, much to the astonishment of my friends, I announced that I was going to join the Navy and become a WAVE.

After testing, I was sworn into the Navy that February and reported to OCS that summer. Much to my amazement, I really enjoyed the program and signed up to be commissioned after my 1964 graduation. I walked in my cap and gown to receive my diploma, disappeared, and came back in my dress whites. You could have heard a pin drop as I walked to the podium to be sworn in.

I reported to my first duty station, Commander, Naval Base San Diego, at the foot of Broadway. I was assigned as a public information officer. My duties included fostering community relations and acting as a liaison with the press. Our offices faced the Navy pier, and we witnessed ship after ship loading up Marines and soldiers heading for South Vietnam.

In August 1964, the notorious Gulf of Tonkin incident occurred off the coast of Vietnam. Two of our destroyers were fired upon by North Vietnamese gunboats. Although United States military personnel had been acting as advisors in South Vietnam, this was the impetus for extended action on the part of the United States. At the time, the idea was to halt the communist invasion and prevent the communism "domino effect" throughout Southeast Asia. This action caused a good deal of anti-war sentiment as well as huge protests here in the United States. These protests often included vicious attacks against military personnel. Luckily, San Diego was a Navy town. In San Diego, the protests were minimal, and our service men and women were supported.

In 1967, I married Commander Roger Usborne, a fellow Navy officer. Roger was stationed in Virginia Beach, so we commuted on weekends. The Navy couldn't seem to be able to station us close to each other. At the time, WAVEs were not allowed to have children, so I just decided the best thing would be to resign. I took off my uniform for the last time in February 1968.

After a six-month tour in Newport, Rhode Island, my husband was ordered to a destroyer in San Diego. The ship deployed to Southeast Asia for six months to support our troops. We had one son at the time, and we bought a small house in Chula Vista, California.

Communication with ships was difficult. Mail took weeks, and there was no internet. Roger could phone when the ship pulled into a port, but the calls were very expensive. After that deployment, Roger became commanding officer of a repair ship that was permanently deployed in South Vietnam to repair the boats being used to fight on the rivers. Our second son was born while he was in Vietnam. I sent him a telegram, but I was home from the hospital before he found out. The Navy wives were very cohesive and supportive during this time. Resentment against the war was mounting, and end points were debated. Many in the Navy felt that the president and secretary of defense were micromanaging the war, and that Navy personnel were not allowed to use the tools needed to win the conflict. It was called a "limited war."

In 1971, Roger received orders to be a liaison officer with the Spanish Navy in Madrid, Spain. We moved to Monterey, California, so he could attend the Defense Language School. We arrived in Madrid in the summer of 1972. There was very limited access to any English language information regarding the conduct of the Vietnam War. We did not personally see the POW's returning home and the end of the conflict. Many believe that the United States should have listened to General MacArthur when he advised that our country should not become involved in a land war in Asia. We did not return to the United States until 1976, and Roger retired from the Navy in 1983. We had a plaque made for the Veterans' Memorial at Mount Soledad in La Jolla, California. I am proud to have been both a Navy officer and Navy wife during this troubling war.

The plaque placed at the Veterans' Memorial, Mount Soledad, La Jolla, California, by Elizabeth and Roger Usborne.

THE WAR FROM AFAR*

By Marion Tanner Wiener
Presidio Chapter, NSDAR
San Francisco, California

April 1, 1956, the first United States women were deployed to Vietnam to train military nurses. I was an eighteen-year-old kid living in Rockford, Illinois. I had already lived through World War II and the Korean Conflict. I didn't know anything about Vietnam. I didn't know where it was, and I didn't know about its history of conflict that first involved the French. Like most young people of my time, I had no idea that my twenties and thirties would be splattered with a war we would not win.

Marion Tanner
San Francisco, 1960.

When the first CIA Agents were sent to Vietnam on December 5, 1960, I was living in San Francisco and was the independent women I hoped and planned to be. In 1961, Secretary of State Dean Rusk and Secretary of Defense Robert McNamara recommended to President John F. Kennedy that "We now make the decision to commit ourselves to the objective of preventing the fall of South Vietnam to Communism and that, in so doing so, we recognize that the introduction of the United States and other SEATO forces may be necessary to achieve this objective." President Kennedy took the advice. Everyone I knew thought this was a huge mistake. Secretary of Defense McNamara finally figured that out and admitted his mistake forty-one years later. Secretary of State Rusk never did.

---

*Dates and incident descripions were taken from the Vietnam War 50th Anniversary Commemoration Timeline, *http://www.vietnamwar50th.com/timeline*.

My male family and friends of draft age feared Vietnam, but, like most young men, they did not leave their country to avoid the draft. They served when their country called. I supported our troops.

By the time President Kennedy was assassinated in Dallas on November 22, 1963, there were 16,900 American military personnel in Vietnam and seventy already had died there. Then the conflict became President Lyndon Johnson's war, a war he micromanaged and escalated. It became one of the cruelest legacies of his presidency, with 58,253 dead, 153,363 injured, and 2,646 missing in action. I didn't personally know anyone who died in the war, was injured or who is still missing in action.

The Vietnam War era was disorderly. I was a generation ahead of the "baby boomers," that large demographic of kids competing with each other for attention, education, jobs, and the American Dream. Most did not riot in the streets, blow things up, hold sit-ins and protests, and disrespect everyone over thirty; but there were enough who did to make life miserable for the rest of us. In San Francisco, many folks were busier with sex, drugs and rock and roll than with Vietnam. However, there were frequent anti-war protests, demonstrations, marches, and sit-ins. Military personnel were insulted and assaulted. They were spit upon by their fellow baby boomers. They quit wearing their uniforms at home. They got no respect, and they were treated like it had been their idea to be drafted.

The war came into our homes on television at dinnertime every night. That was new. We had lost our ability not to know what war was like. I learned new terms like "Green Beret," "Agent Orange," "Tet," "Medevac," "Hanoi Hilton" and "PTSD."

The war dragged on and on until, finally, the United States admitted it was not willing to win. Secretary of State Henry Kissinger and President Richard Nixon negotiated a settlement, but even that was not without an argument about the shape of the negotiating table. Direct negotiations began on August 4, 1969. We were greatly encouraged when it was announced on October 26, 1972, that, "Peace is at hand." Twenty-five years had passed since President Harry S. Truman committed the first money, advisors, and supplies to Vietnam. On May 12, 1975, we were out of there.

In 2000, I visited Da Nang and Hue. As I rode over the mountain, through the rice paddies, and past small villages, I was taken by how much Vietnam looked exactly as television cameras had captured it. It was the same, except for the haunting sounds of helicopter blades, guns, bombs, the spectacle of burning villages, and wounded and dead bodies. There are cemeteries everywhere in

Marion Tanner Wiener, 2015.

Vietnam. Some cover entire hillsides. A woman on our bus said, "So far, I haven't seen one thing that is worth one American life."

During the Vietnam War, I thought that it would be "the war to end all wars," as had been hoped in World War I. It wasn't. Since then, I have lived through several more with expectations of more to come. It is my opinion that only one good thing came out of the Vietnam War: The War Powers Resolution:

> *The constitutional powers of the President as Commander-in-Chief to introduce United States Armed Forces into hostilities, or into situations where imminent involvement in hostilities is clearly indicated by the circumstances, are exercised only pursuant to (1) a declaration of war, (2) specific statutory authorization, or (3) a national emergency created by attack upon the United States, its territories or possessions, or its armed forces."*

All United States presidents swear to uphold this resolution, but they don't. Sending military personnel to train foreign personnel was how we got into the Vietnam War. "Those who can't remember the past are condemned to repeat it."

SERVICE WITH THE USO

By Debbie Balsley Williams
Letitia Coxe Shelby Chapter, NSDAR
La Mesa, California

In the 1960's, Bob Hope's Christrnas specials always ended with his asking young ladies, ages of eighteen to twenty-five, to volunteer time to the USO. Young ladies were always needed to talk and dance with the many active military that were off duty in their home town USO's. I guess Mr. Hope asked so many times, I felt obligated to do something about it. In my family, I had one brother serving in the Air Force, and brothers-in-law serving in the Navy and Marines. I also had one cousin flying in helicopters over Vietnam and two others flying planes. Duty called!

Debbie Balsley, 1968.

With a few of my girlfriends from our class of 1967, we joined the USO Junior Volunteer crew. All of us had college plans, so for that one summer we felt we could do something to help. It would turn out to be a very rewarding opportunity for all of us.

There were dances three nights a week and card tournaments on Mondays. We served dinners on Tuesdays and Sundays. There was something to do everyday to keep our military from being extremely bored or from getting into trouble.

I went to school downtown and was out before 2:00 p.m., so I would just go to the club, do my homework there before anyone came in and then be there for whatever was going on. I loved doing it all - chatting, serving dinners, dancing, playing cards, and going on outings to Balboa Park.

For me, helping out at the Balboa Naval Hospital on Sundays was very trying, but a good learning experience. I pushed the wounded in wheelchairs uphill from the hospital to Balboa Park to play dominos or cards. For four or five hours at a time, I wrote letters on behalf of the blind patients. Keeping an upbeat tone while doing this service was taxing, to say the least. The wounded didn't like to talk too much about how they were injured, and we didn't ask. Mostly, we just wanted them to just keep good faith that they would get better and return to their hometowns, to their families and friends. We figured if we could get one patient out of the hospital for a few hours of fresh San Diego air and good company, it was worth it.

The dances were three times a week. They were grueling for us girls. There were usually only sixteen to twenty young ladies to dance with 100 or more wonderful guys in a basement with no windows and just a few big fans. Only one dance at a time for each serviceman. We had a six-inch distance rule for slow dancing. The laughs we got for that rule! The senior volunteers did keep those rules enforced, coming around with the dreaded six-inch ruler to check. Funny yes, but those volunteers were adamant about keeping us all in line. Good thing too, now that I remember some instances of inappropriate behavior.

Our Navy DJ's - Rick, Scratch, and Leprechaun - all watched out for us girls. They made sure we didn't overdo it. Boy, could they pick the songs. Remember, the 1960's had everything: the jerk, stroll, twist, pony, monkey, hully gully, watusi, hitchhike, monster mash, swim, freddie, and the swing (yes, we were still doing that). We loved it all, and we learned so much. Not only did we dance the night away, but experiencing personalities from all over the United States was wonderful. All the servicemen talked about their hometowns and their girlfriends. I loved the accents and always tried to figure out where they were from. I usually missed by a few states.

The experience proved monumental for a few of us who committed to a year or more of service. The emotional rollercoaster of meeting new friends from all over the United States - laughing, playing cards, dancing, talking, and having a good time - would dampen sharply a few months later when we learned of untimely deaths.

Debbie Balsley Williams, 2013.

It was extremely heartbreaking and emotionally brutal. However, we knew we had to keep going back because we were needed by those sailors and Marines, who kept coming back to the USO for a little chat or dance before they were deployed to Vietnam.

I hope in some small way, we Junior Volunteers made a difference to these brave, young men. We loved all of the wonderful servicemen we met, the characters, the delightful personalities. We will never forget them. As for me, I learned we can never do enough for our active military and our veterans. My tour of USO volunteering lasted from June 1967 to January 1969. I received a 1,000-hour volunteer USO pin for my service.

MY BRACELET

By Linda Wood
El Paso de Robles Chapter, NSDAR
Paso Robles, California

During the Vietnam War, many Americans wore bracelets with the names of MIA/POW military personnel engraved on them. My family and many of my friends wore those bracelets. It was a way of honoring the men and women fighting in Vietnam and keeping them in our thoughts and prayers. For me, wearing the bracelet made the war a little more personal.

Bracelet worn by Linda Wood

I wore a bracelet for Lieutenant David G. Rehmann, United States Navy. He was taken as a prisoner of war when his plane was shot down on December 2, 1966. He was held captive for over six years. The communists used a propaganda film showing him being marched through a war crimes tribunal. His face was burned and swollen, and, he had a broken arm. This picture was used in advertisements from the United States government in advertisements to show the way the communists treated the POW's. He was released February 12, 1973. I wore Lieutenant Rehmann's bracelet 24-7 until the day he returned home.

Lieutenant David G. Rehmann, POW, 1966.

When Lieutenant Rehmann returned home, I wrote to him, thanking him for his service, to tell him how happy I was that he survived and that he had been in my prayers. Lieutenant Rehmann sent me a letter and a photograph.

Photograph from Lieutenant David G. Rehmann, to Linda Wood, 1973.

On April 30, 1974, Lieutenant Rehmann was medically retired from the Navy. At that time, a citizens group organized to elect David Rehmann to Congress from California's new 38th District. This district includes Garden Grove, the city that adopted him while in prison to demonstrate America's broad concern for POW's.

Dear Linda

I sincerely apologize for not having replied to your letter as quickly as I had originally planned. However, as you can imagine, my daily existence has been extremley hectic since my return home and the volume of mail I've received has been overwhelming. Nevertheless, it has been a wonderful experience to read all the warm greetings from people as far away as Maine and Hawaii.

You are probably wondering what kind of guy would survive over six years of captivity? Well, the doctors at least tell me I'm quite normal and in good health. I am happy to report I agree whole-heartedly. I was born April 27, 1942 in Bay City, Michigan and in 1950 my family and I moved to Los Angeles. Subsequent relocations took the "Rehmanns" to Culver City and Lancaster, California and in 1964 I signed a four year contract with the Navy to become a Radar Intercept Officer.

I have four brothers and one sister and although my father is deceased, my mother resides in San Diego, California. I am single, interested in "girls", sports, music, plays and literature. My personal hobbies are tennis, golf, skiing, scuba diving and sailing.

Presently I am attached to Balboa Naval Hospital. I am planning to take 90 days leave very soon and return to the Hospital for some corrective surgery on my arm.

For the moment, I have no immediate plans for my future. However, while I am on leave, I am going to try to determine whether or not to continue my Naval career and to investigate some civilian job opportunities. I also intend to explore the possibility of going back to school.

On a more serious note, our country has had a tough job to do in Vietnam, and that job has yet to be completed. I personally feel that it is America's job to lead the Free World and this is never an easy task. I believe in America and I am very proud to have served in her armed forces. I was fairly young when I was shot down and I feel that my time spent in Hanoi was for all Americans and especially for the youth in our country. War is a hardship on everyone and I hope that today's generation of young people will never have to experience combat and become prisoners of war sometime in their future.

I want to thank you for your warm concern and interest. May God Bless you and I shall remember you in my prayers.

Sincerely,

David G. Rehmann
LT, USNR

Letter from Lieutenant David G. Rehmann to Linda Wood, 1973.

A MOTHER'S PERSPECTIVE

By Doris Wright
Captain Henry Sweetser Chapter, NSDAR
Santa Maria, California

What? Another war? The Vietnam War brought back memories of WWII, the second war that was to "end all wars." That was a time when my parents listened to the radio many hours a day for news of my seventeen-year-old brother (serving in the Navy in the Pacific), my uncle (serving in the Army in Germany), and several friends who were serving in distant lands. As a young adult, the Korean War seemed somewhat more distant to me, but I was still concerned about that conflict involving our military.

Fast forward to the Vietnam War era. I was a mother of four. During that time, the draft board changed to a new lottery system based on birth dates. The number "nineteen" was drawn from the lottery. This was my son Scott's birthdate, so his draft number was nineteen.

In the spring of 1971, Scott, who was not quite twenty years old, received his draft notice. Now this brought the war into my house. After much discussion and thought about his low draft number, my son enlisted in the Army for two years, June 1971. He was sent to Fort Lewis,

Private Scott Wright
United State Army

Washington, for basic training. Then he was assigned to the Air Defense & Ground Artillery at Fort Bliss, Texas. Training for duty in Vietnam began immediately. It quickly became clear to me why my folks listened daily to the radio during WWII. I found myself repeating the same pattern with added pictures of the

Vietnam War brought into my home via television.

While at Fort Bliss, Scott volunteered for the Military Funeral Detail. It was an honor for him to serve as each veteran, some fallen in the line of duty in Vietnam, was given an honorable burial. These veterans had served their country well. At each burial service, Scott realized how quickly life can end, regardless of age or circumstance.

At the end of his two-year enlistment, Scott was discharged without having to serve in Vietnam. The Vietnam War era was a difficult time for our country, particularly for families that lost loved ones. Scott answered his call to duty, and his memories linger as to the ultimate price many veterans paid during the Vietnam War.

INDEX

214

Made in the USA
San Bernardino, CA
10 July 2016